MANCHESTER UNITED FOOTBALL ANNUAL 2001

OFFICIAL MERCHANDISE

Written and compiled by Jeremy Paxton

First published in 2000 by Manchester United Books, André Deutsch Ltd, 76 Dean Street, London W1V 5HA.

Design by Brown Wells and Jacobs Ltd. Foresters Hall, 25/27 Westow Street, London SE19 3RY.
Tel: 020 8771 5115. Fax: 020 8771 9994.

A catalogue record for this title is available from the British Library.

ISBN 0 233 99622 2.

Reprographics by TWA Limited. Printed by PROOST NV, The Netherlands.

HOW TO USE YOUR FLIXPIX!

On every right hand page of this annual there are frames taken from a piece of live action. To make them come to life, simply use your thumb to bend back the pages from Page 64 to the front and then steadily pull back your thumb to let the pages flick over.

CONTENTS

Roll of Honour

European Champion Club's Cup Winners - 2
1968, 1999

European Cup Winner's Cup Winners - 1
1991

European Super Cup Winners - 1
1991

Intercontinental Cup Winners - 1
1999

FA Premier League Champions - 6
1993, 1994, 1996, 1997, 1999, 2000

FA Premier League Runners-Up - 2
1995, 1998

Division 1 Champions - 7
1908, 1911, 1952, 1956, 1957, 1965, 1967

Division 1 Runners Up - 10
1947, 1948, 1949, 1951, 1959,
1964, 1968, 1980, 1988, 1992

FA Cup Winners - 10
1909, 1948, 1963, 1977, 1983,
1985, 1990, 1994, 1996, 1999

FA Cup Runners Up - 5
1957, 1958, 1976, 1979, 1995

League Cup Winners - 1
1992

League Cup Runners Up - 3
1983, 1991, 1994

FA Charity Shield Winners - 10
1908, 1911, 1952, 1956, 1957,
1983, 1993, 1994, 1996, 1997

FA Charity Shield Joint Holders - 4
1965, 1967, 1977, 1990

'Double' Winners – Premier League & FA Cup - 2
1994, 1996

'Treble' Winners – Premier League, FA Cup & European Champion's Cup - 1
1999

FA Youth Cup Winners - 8
1953, 1954, 1955, 1956,
1957, 1965, 1992, 1995

BEHIND THE SCENES

MANCHESTER UNITED PLC, OLD TRAFFORD, MANCHESTER M16 0RA

Manager: Sir Alex Ferguson CBE
Coach: Steven McLaren
Physio: Robert Swire
Kit Manager: Albert Morgan
Reserve Manager: Jim Ryan
Youth Manager: Eric Harrison
Chief Executive & Chairman: C.M. Edwards
Directors: C.M. Edwards, Sir Bobby Charlton CBE,
J.M. Edelson, E.M. Watkins Ll.M., R.L. Olive, P.F. Kenyon, D.A. Gill
Club Secretary: Kenneth Merrett
Main Switchboard: 0161 868 8000
Ticket & Match Info (24 hour): 0161 868 8020
Official Website: http://WWW.MANUTD.COM

All information correct at time of going to press

STAT ATTACK

Founded: 1878
Stadium: Old Trafford
Capacity: 67,500 (approx)
Pitch Size: 116 x 76 yards
Nickname: Red Devils
Main Sponsors: Vodafone
Kit Sponsors: Umbro
Record attendance: 70,504 v Aston Villa, Division 1, 27/12/1920
Record League Victory: 10 - 1 v Wolves, Division 1, 15 /10/1892
Record Cup Victory: 10 - 0 v Anderlecht, European Cup. 26/9/1956
Record Appearances: Bobby Charlton (756 between 1956 & 1973)
Record Goalscorer: Bobby Charlton (199 between 1956 & 1973)
Record Transfer in: £12.6M (Dwight Yorke from Aston Villa, 1998)
Record Transfer out: £7M (Paul Ince to Inter Milan, 1995)

SPOT the BALL

We have removed the ball from the picture below. Take a close look and use your football skill to judge where the centre of the ball should be. Then use the grid to get a co-ordinate for the square the ball has been removed from (for example: A1).

	A	B	C	D	E	F	G	H	
1									1
2									2
3									3
4									4
5									5
6									6
7									7
8									8
	A	B	C	D	E	F	G	H	

FAST FACT

United legend Bobby Charlton is the England national team's all-time leading goalscorer with a grand total of 49 goals.

CHECK PAGE 64 FOR THE ANSWER TO SEE IF YOU ARE RIGHT!

Enter the THEATRE OF DREAMS

The Old Trafford Stadium has been home to some of the world's best footballers; from the great 'Busby Babes' of the 1950s and George Best in the 1970s, right up to Alex Ferguson's current team of United superstars. However, it is not just the four different types of grass seed used for the pitch that make Old Trafford special, the 'Theatre of Dreams' is much, much more than just somewhere to play football ...

1 THE PITCH

Beneath the pitch are miles of pipes to heat up and defrost the pitch in cold weather and there are three underground springs and a 55,000 gallon water tank under the East Stand keep the grass watered during dry spells. In order to protect the playing surface, no one is allowed on the grass at any time – apart from the players that is!

Manchester United's average attendance is the highest of any football club in England!

2 THE STANDS
An incredible 67,500 (approx) people can sit and watch United in comfort in the South, East, West and North Stands which completely surround the pitch. Beneath the stands are conference rooms, suites and executive boxes. When the ground is full, which is the case for the vast majority of United games, the atmosphere is electric!

3 THE DRESSING ROOMS
Manchester United's home dressing room is huge and contains a spa pool, baths, showers, toilets and a separate warm-up area. Nearby is the players' lounge, where the team relaxes before and after each home game.

4 POLICE CONTROL ROOM
With such an immense stadium, security is of the utmost importance. From the control room, the police can view the entire ground, inside and out, through 27 screens linked to cameras placed at strategic points. A medical team is also available at a second's notice.

5 TV GANTRY
This is where the television match commentators like John Motson and Martin Tyler watch the game. It is high up on the South Stand and gives them a perfect view of the action.

6 MUFC RADIO STATION
From here match commentaries are broadcast to radios within 10 miles of Old Trafford.

4

8

7 THE MEGASTORE
The brand new Manchester United Megastore at Old Trafford opened in the summer and is the largest of its kind in the country. Its 18,000 square feet are packed full of an amazing array of United goodies. See Page 58 for more details on the massive range of official Manchester United merchandise available.

8 THE MUSEUM
The Club Museum has three floors containing everything there is to know about United. It includes the Hall of Fame and the Trophy room where you can see the Premier League trophy and there is also an interactive floor where you can pick your own United dream team.

9 THE RED CAFÉ
Open every non-match day from 9am to 6pm, the Red Café is Manchester United's official themed restaurant where you can eat great food while watching uninterrupted video footage of the Red Devils in action.

10 LAUNDRY
A very important part of any football club! The laundry is where the Kit Manager, Albert Morgan, takes the strips after every game. After all, when our team is winning we want them to look good as well!

DID YOU KNOW? ... On non-match days, you can take a behind-the-scenes tour of Old Trafford, walk down the players' tunnel, sit in the dugout, see the dressing rooms and dream of scoring the winning goal at the Stretford End. Call the Manchester United Museum and Tour Centre on **0161 868 8631** for more details.

REDS on the RAMPAGE

Nicky Butt takes on Saints' Matt le Tissier

Paul Scholes rises high at Chelsea

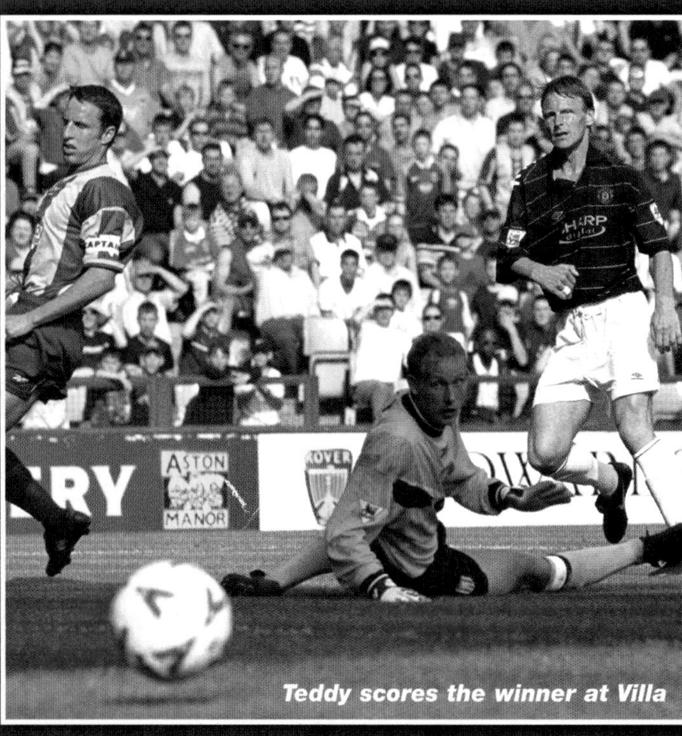

Teddy scores the winner at Villa

FAST FACT

The biggest ever crowd to attend Old Trafford saw a game which didn't even involve United! 76, 962 spectators saw Wolves play Grimsby in an FA Cup Semi-Final in 1939.

FLIXPIX

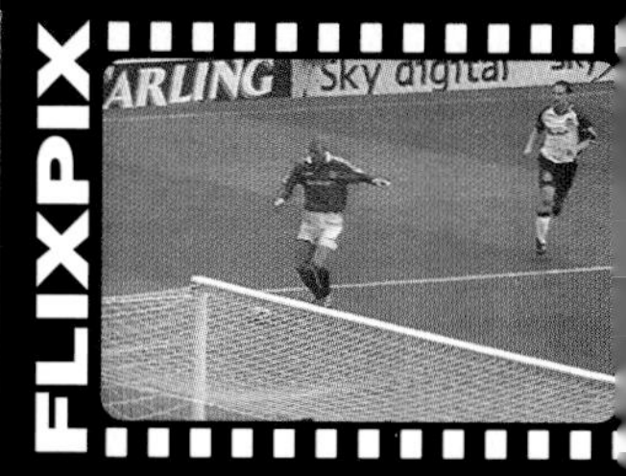

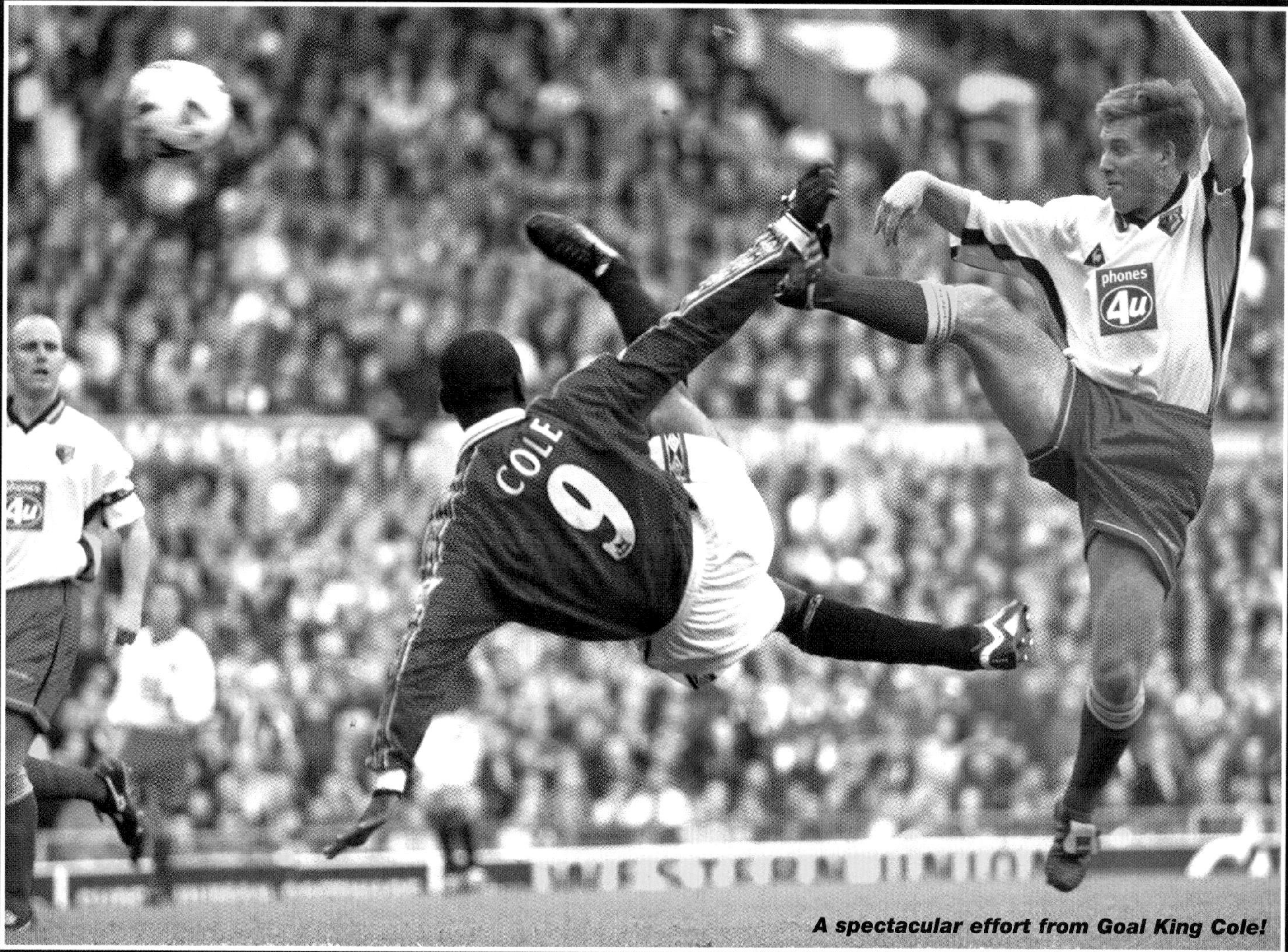

A spectacular effort from Goal King Cole!

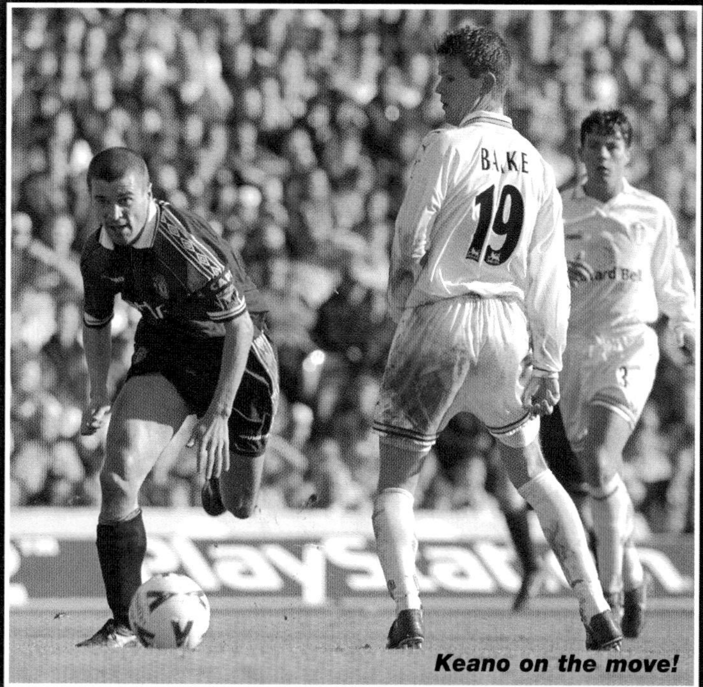

Keano on the move!

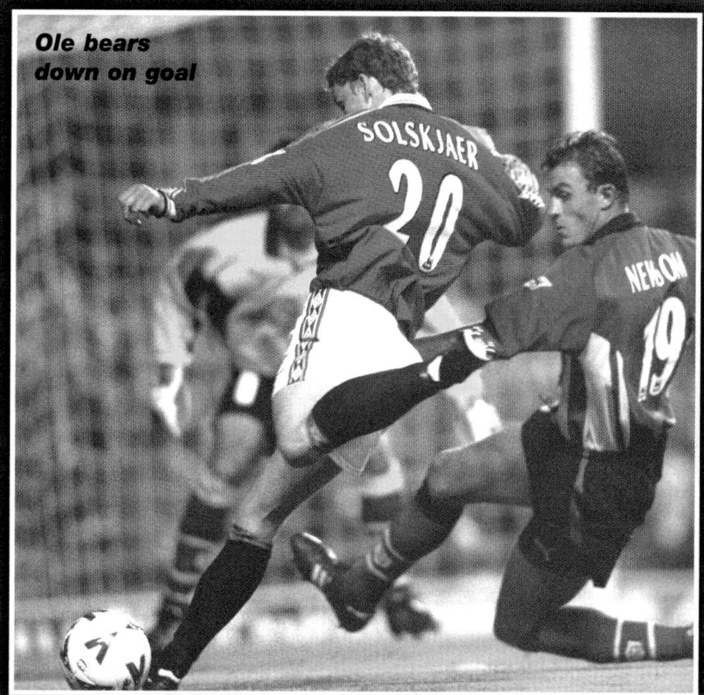

Ole bears down on goal

Where in the

As Manchester United is fanatically supported across the globe, it is not surprising that the team itself comes from all over the world, as you can see in the map! Of the 36 members of the current First Team squad, 16 were born in England, 5 in the Republic of Ireland, 3 in Norway, 2 in Holland, 2 in France and 1 each in Australia, Sweden, South Africa, Wales, Scotland, USA, Italy and Trinidad and Tobago — and, of course, the manager Sir Alex Ferguson is from Scotland!!

UNITED STATES

Paul Rachubka

REPUBLIC OF IRELAND

David Healy
Denis Irwin
Roy Keane
John O'Shea
Lee Roche

TRINIDAD AND TOBAGO

Dwight Yorke

WALES

Ryan Giggs

ENGLAND

David Beckham
Wes Brown
Nicky Butt
Luke Chadwick
Michael Clegg
Andy Cole
Nick Culkin
Jonathan Greening
David May
Gary Neville
Philip Neville
Paul Scholes
Teddy Sheringham
Michael Twiss
Ronnie Wallwork
Mark Wilson

World?

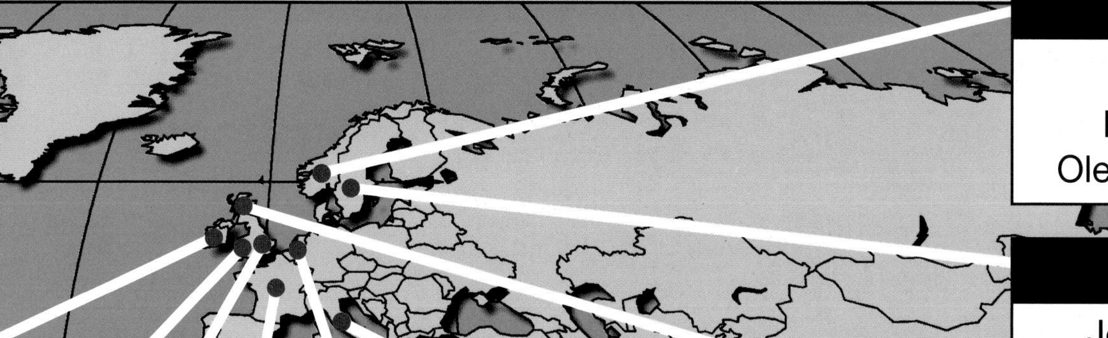

NORWAY
Henning Berg
Ronny Johnsen
Ole Gunnar Solskjaer

SWEDEN
Jesper Blomquist

SCOTLAND
Sir Alex Ferguson
Alex Notman

ITALY
Massimo Taibi

FRANCE
Mikael Silvestre
Fabien Barthez

THE NETHERLANDS
Jaap Stam
Raimond Van Der Gouw

SOUTH AFRICA
Quinton Fortune

AUSTRALIA
Mark Bosnich

It's a funny old game!

Imagine you are Sir Alex Ferguson and have just given the United players their final team-talk and sent them onto the Old Trafford pitch for an all-important Champion's League encounter against Juventus or Barcelona. Now all you can do is watch and hope that your preparations will prove enough against the cream of world football ... or is it? With just a little imagination and a couple of dice, you can recreate all the excitement of football with this game that you can play on your own or with a friend.

YOU WILL NEED – Two dice (preferably of different colours) and pen and paper (to keep the score!).

BEFORE YOU START – Decide which of the two dice will be Dice 1 and which will be Dice 2 – this is very important!

FOR TWO PLAYERS – If you are playing with a friend, decide who is going to kick off by tossing a coin. The winner of the toss will now be PLAYER 1, while the loser is PLAYER 2. PLAYER 1 starts and will be 'in possession of the ball'. PLAYER 1 throws both dice at the same time. When they have stopped rolling, refer to the table below to see what happened in this passage of play. If the result of the throw is 'keep possession' then PLAYER 1 should throw the dice again and play continues until the result of the throw is 'lose possession'. At this point, PLAYER 2 'takes possession of the ball' and throws the dice, following the instructions below until he loses possession.

SCORING A GOAL – When the dice are thrown and the result is a GOAL, then whoever has possession has scored a goal. Make a note on your piece of paper of the current score and possession passes to the other player who now 'kicks-off' and play continues as before.

TIMING – There are many ways of deciding how long each game should be, you could play until your tea is ready, for example. However, probably the best way is to decide a target of, say, 5 or 10 goals, and as soon as one of you has reached this number the game is over. If you have a watch or even a stopwatch you can play for a set period of time, say 5 minutes, although you will have to be careful about time-wasting as the match draws to an end! You could also play for two halves with PLAYER 2 kicking off the second half.

FOR ONE PLAYER – In order to play on your own then you should follow the instructions for the two-player game, although, of course, you will be both players at the same time and will throw the dice regardless of who is in possession. To make things a little easier and more fun imagine that the two different PLAYERS are teams that you know (for example, Manchester United and Liverpool) and remember which team has possession of the ball as you play.

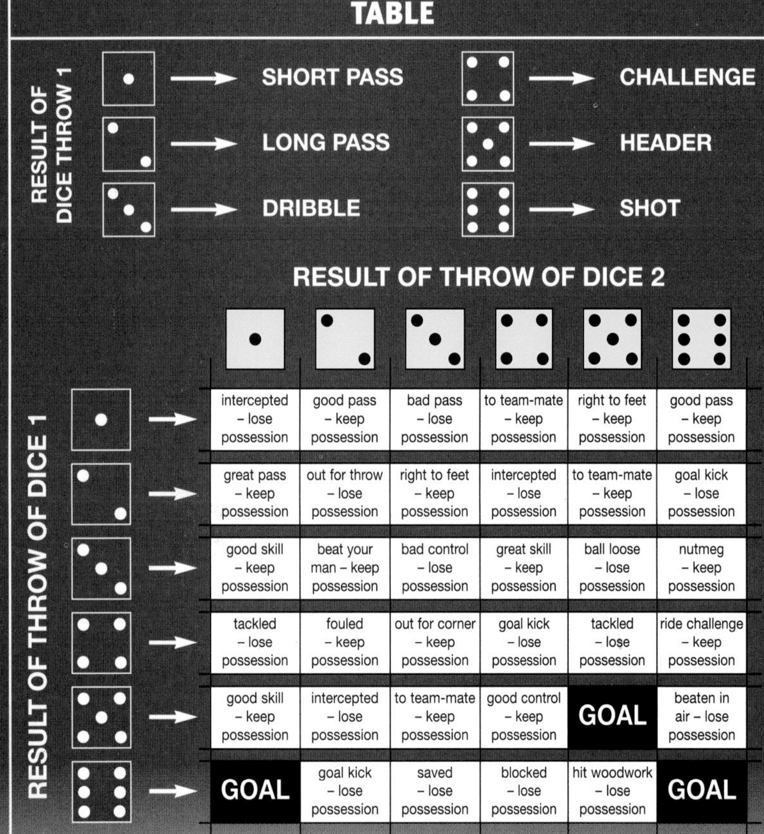

TABLE

RESULT OF DICE THROW 1

Dice 1	Result	Dice 1	Result
1	SHORT PASS	4	CHALLENGE
2	LONG PASS	5	HEADER
3	DRIBBLE	6	SHOT

RESULT OF THROW OF DICE 2

RESULT OF THROW OF DICE 1	1	2	3	4	5	6
1	intercepted – lose possession	good pass – keep possession	bad pass – lose possession	to team-mate – keep possession	right to feet – keep possession	good pass – keep possession
2	great pass – keep possession	out for throw – lose possession	right to feet – keep possession	intercepted – lose possession	to team-mate – keep possession	goal kick – lose possession
3	good skill – keep possession	beat your man – keep possession	bad control – lose possession	great skill – keep possession	ball loose – lose possession	nutmeg – keep possession
4	tackled – lose possession	fouled – keep possession	out for corner – keep possession	goal kick – lose possession	tackled – lose possession	ride challenge – keep possession
5	good skill – keep possession	intercepted – lose possession	to team-mate – keep possession	good control – keep possession	GOAL	beaten in air – lose possession
6	GOAL	goal kick – lose possession	saved – lose possession	blocked – lose possession	hit woodwork – lose possession	GOAL

FOR EXAMPLE

Here, PLAYER 1 has possession of the ball and play continues as below:

	Dice 1	Dice 2	
THROW 1	1	5	SHORT PASS – RIGHT TO FEET – KEEP POSSESSION
THROW 2	3	6	DRIBBLE – NUTMEG DEFENDER – KEEP POSSESSION
THROW 3	3	2	DRIBBLE – BEAT YOUR MAN – KEEP POSSESSION
THROW 4	4	3	CHALLENGE – OUT FOR CORNER – KEEP POSSESSION
THROW 5	2	5	LONG PASS – TO TEAM-MATE – KEEP POSSESSION
THROW 6	5	5	HEADER – • GOAL • – LOSE POSSESSION (PLAYER 2 KICKS OFF)
THROW 7	1	2	SHORT PASS – GOOD PASS – KEEP POSSESSION (PLAYER 2)

Continue play in this way until the end of the game ... HAVE FUN!

United Word Grid

Find the 25 words below in the United Word Grid. When you've spotted them all, see if y can work out the famous four word phrase which describes Manchester United perfect by reading the unused letters from top left to bottom right! The answer is on Page 64

BALL	COLE	GIGGS	NEVILLE	SCHOLES
BARTHEZ	CORNER	GOAL	OFFSIDE	SHOT
BECKHAM	CROSS	HEADER	PENALTY	SILVESTR
BERG	FERGUSON	IRWIN	PREMIERSHIP	STAM
BUTT	FREE KICK	KEANE	SAVE	YORKE

P	E	N	A	L	T	Y	S	G	G	I	G	B
N	R	T	T	U	B	U	Y	O	R	K	E	A
I	S	E	S	I	L	V	E	S	T	R	E	R
W	S	T	M	H	N	E	N	A	E	K	F	T
R	O	I	A	I	O	F	F	S	I	D	E	H
I	R	T	E	M	E	T	D	A	R	E	R	E
K	C	I	K	E	E	R	F	L	A	O	G	Z
S	R	E	D	A	E	H	S	T	H	E	U	C
A	B	H	A	S	E	L	O	H	C	S	S	G
V	A	N	E	V	I	L	L	E	I	M	O	R
E	L	O	C	O	R	N	E	R	P	P	N	E
I	L	B	E	C	K	H	A	M	O	N	S	B

GOLDEN BOY BECKS

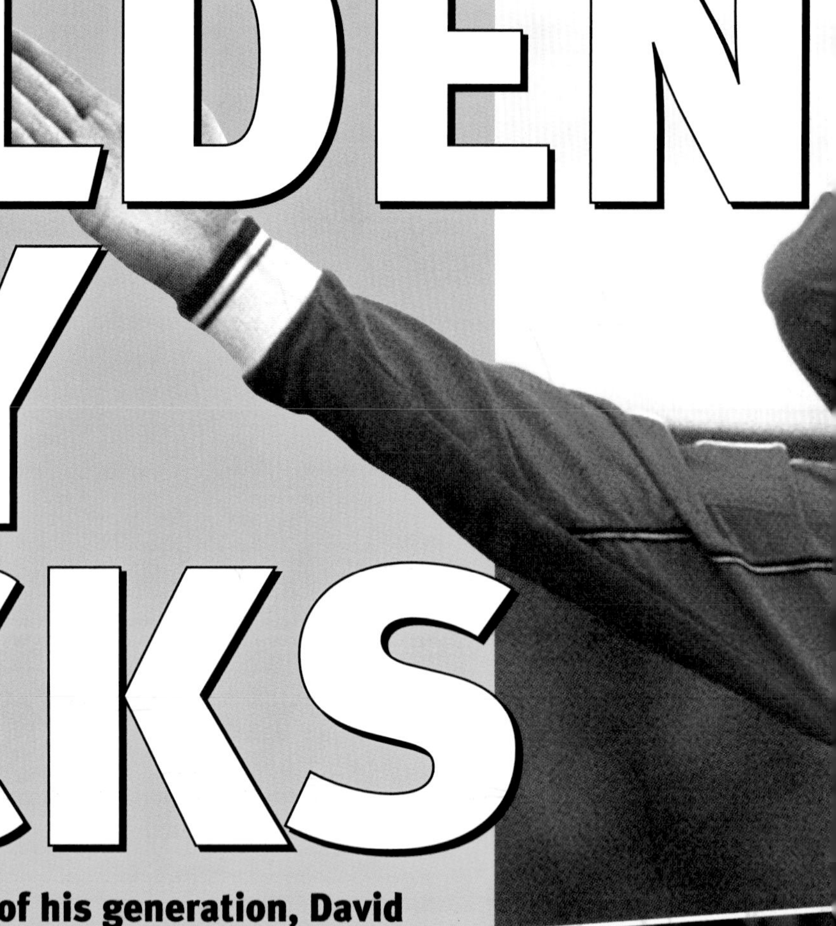

Probably the most gifted footballer of his generation, David Beckham's rise to world-wide fame with both Manchester United and England is the stuff dreams are made of.

Born in Leytonstone, London, David had trials with Leyton Orient and attended Tottenham Hotspurs' School of Excellence before signing for United as a trainee in July 1991. Less than a year into his United career, Becks collected the first of his many medals when the Manchester United Youth team (which also included Paul Scholes, Nicky Butt and the Neville brothers) lifted the FA Youth Cup in May 1992. Five months later, David got his first taste of First Team action as he came on as substitute for twenty minutes in the Rumbelows Cup (now the Worthington Cup) second round away tie at Brighton on 1 October 1992.

It would be another two years before Becks appeared for the First Team again, when he scored at Old Trafford in the UEFA Champion's League against Galatasary on 7 December 1994. The following season (1995-96) Becks helped United secure an historic second League and FA Cup double – the 'Double Double'. David had become an established regular in the team and his fantastic performances and outstanding goals in the 1996-97 season, including his famous goal from the halfway line at Selhurst Park against Wimbledon, brought him a call up to the full England squad and his first cap in September 1997 versus Moldova. Becks had become a household name and was heading towards international superstardom.

The 1997-98 season was ultimately frustrating for United as Arsenal claimed the League title and FA Cup. Even so, Becks' form continued to be outstanding and the whole country eagerly awaited that summer's World Cup Finals in France. The then England Manager, Glenn Hoddle, at first refused to play David, preferring the experience of Spurs' Darren Anderton. However, when Becks did play, in the make or

Continued on Page 16

THE BEST RIGHT FOOT IN THE WORLD!

Most football experts would agree that David Beckham's whipped right-footed crosses and deadly accurate set pieces have been vital to Manchester United's recent domination of the game in both England and Europe. This has become Becks' trademark – he wraps his foot right around the ball and drives the ball with such power and accuracy into the heart of the penalty area that it is almost impossible to defend. He also scores his fair share of goals – some from spectacular free kicks and some when he bursts into the penalty area to finish off another quality United move. With the superb service provided by Becks, it is no wonder that Andy Cole and Dwight Yorke play the game with smiles on their faces.

SOME SAY THAT DAVID BECKHAM HAS IT ALL ...

- ❑ He plays football for Manchester United (not only the biggest football club in the world but also the team he supported as a boy)
- ❑ He earns vast sums of money for playing the game he loves
- ❑ He is a regular member of the full England squad
- ❑ He is married to the beautiful and equally successful Victoria Adams (who is, of course, Posh Spice from the Spice Girls)
- ❑ He is the proud father of baby Brooklyn

break group match against Colombia, he showed the whole world what he could do with a wonderful 25-yard free kick goal. Indeed, this helped ensure England's progression to the Second Stage of the tournament.

It was in the following game against Argentina that David's world class status was established, although it was difficult to see it that way at the time. At half time the score was 2-2 after 45 minutes of pulsating action which included Michael Owen's wondergoal which was started with an inch perfect through ball from David Beckham. Early into the second period, Becks clashed with Diego Simeone and a petulant flick of the right leg earned him the first red card of his career. While his England team-mates should have won the game before penalties, David Batty's missed spot-kick saw England crash out of the World Cup. The tabloids turned on Becks with a ferocity not seen before, blaming him for England's World Cup exit and questioning his relationship and "pop star" lifestyle with "Posh Spice", Victoria Adams. It was a difficult time, and there were rumours all summer that David would turn tail and run, joining an Italian or Spanish team to escape the British media. But Beckham proved he had come of age, as he lined up with the rest of his Manchester United colleagues for the start of the memorable 1998-99 season, scoring in the first league game against Leicester.

By the following May, United had won the FA Cup, the Premier League and, on that magical night in Barcelona against Bayern Munich, the European Cup — thus clinching the awesome Treble! An extravagant wedding and the birth of baby Brooklyn saw David on the front pages again, while on the field, he was showing increasingly assured and mature performances both for United and England. Not only that, but Becks had answered all his critics with some of the best football of his career and was voted United's Player of the Year by the fans.

With the media spotlight on football ever more intense, it seems that Becks can never escape attention. Whether it be his reported wish to play in a more central midfield role, his fashion sense, his hairstyle, his sending off in the FIFA World Club Champions Cup, the reported £10,000 he spent on Brooklyn's first birthday party or his possible transfer to a club nearer his Hertfordshire home, he never seems to be off either the front or back pages of the newspapers.

The 1999-2000 season saw Becks finish second only to Brazil's Rivaldo as FIFA World Footballer of the Year and consistently turn in match-winning performances as United cruised to the Premier League title and Kevin Keegan, the new England manager, has made him an automatic choice in England's midfield. David also scored his 50th goal in a United shirt in the 3-1 Premier League victory over Spurs at Old Trafford. It seems that we may not have seen the best yet from the East London boy who made it good in Manchester! ●

DAVID BECKHAM

Full Name: David Joseph Beckham
Position: Midfield
Nickname: Becks
Date of Birth: 2 May 1975
Place of Birth: Leytonstone, London
Height: 6' 0"
Weight: 11st. 11lb.
Previous Clubs: Preston North End (on loan)
United Debut: vs Brighton
at Goldstone Ground 23/9/92 (League Cup)
First United Goal: vs Galatasary
at Old Trafford 7/12/94 (Champion's League)
Total United Appearances: 230 (+23 as sub)
Total United Goals: 50

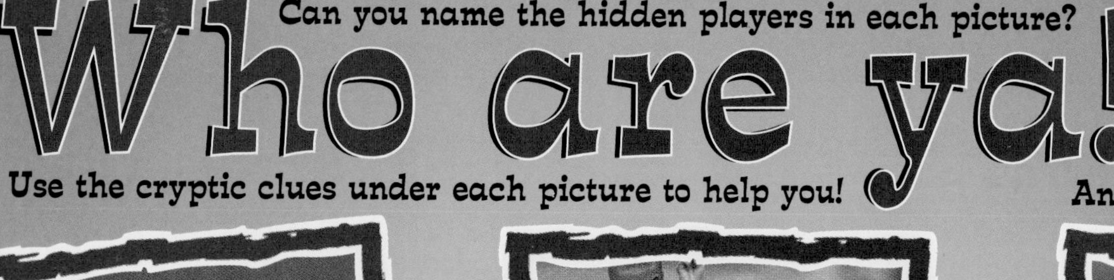

Can you name the hidden players in each picture?

Use the cryptic clues under each picture to help you!

Answers on Page 64

FLIXPIX

1 Who is giving Dwight Yorke all the 'backing' he needs?

2 Which United star is having to live 'hand to mouth'?

3 Who is performing mid-air acrobatics?

4 This keeper doesn't seem too 'keen' to tangle with this United player!

5 Who is David May helping to stoop to conquer?

6 Colin Jackson look out! Your countryman looks to have mastered hurdling!

1 ---------------------------- 3 ---------------------------- 5 ----------------------------

2 ---------------------------- 4 ---------------------------- 6 ----------------------------

Scholes directs a header towards the Valencia goal

UNITED IN

Coley in acrobatic mood again!

FAST FACT

When Sir Matt Busby's Manchester United team beat Benfica 4-1 in the European Cup Final in 1968 they became the first ever English side to lift the famous trophy!

Denis Irwin turns away from trouble!

Yorkey shields the ball in the ill-fated match with Real Madrid

EUROPE

Roy Keane uses his head against Fiorentina

SHARPSHOOTER

When Alex Ferguson broke United's transfer record to bring Dwight Yorke to Old Trafford, many thought it a mistake. How wrong can you be?

If any footballer can be said to play the game "with a smile on his face" then it must be Dwight Yorke. With his unmistakable bright white cycling shorts and laid back attitude, Yorke has forged an awesome striking partnership with Andy Cole which amassed 50 goals in their first season together following his record breaking £12.6 million transfer from Aston Villa in August 1998.

Dwight Yorke was born on 3 November 1971 on the island of Tobago and grew up playing his football under the hot Caribbean sun. Comparisons with the Brazilians practising their footballing skills on Copacabana beach in Rio de Janeiro are obvious, and Yorkey's eye for goal and sublime ball skills are reminiscent of the very best of the South Americans. It was Graham Taylor who first spotted the emerging talent of Dwight Yorke while on a friendly tour of the West Indies as Manager of Aston Villa. In 1989, when he was 17, Dwight swapped the Caribbean for Birmingham as he joined Villa from St Clairs for £120,000. A year later, he made his full league debut against, would you believe it, Manchester United at Old Trafford on 29 December 1990. It was no dream debut for Dwight as he failed to score, but his team earned a creditable 1-1 draw.

Shortly afterwards, Ron Atkinson took over as Villa boss, as Graham Taylor was now the England Manager, and for the next three years Yorke found himself out of favour through injury and the good form of his striking colleagues. Unfortunately, he missed out on Villa's 3-1 victory over United in the 1994 Coca-Cola (League) Cup Final but made up for it by scoring in the 1996 Final, collecting a winner's medal. He went on to become the club's leading scorer in the next two seasons with 20 goals in 1996/97 and 16 in 1997/98 — the form which persuaded Sir Alex Ferguson to chase his signature, but it would not be easy.

Aston Villa's new Manager, John Gregory, was desperate to keep his star striker, especially after selling Dwight's forward partner Dion Dublin to Coventry. It was only when Yorkey himself expressed his desire to join United that the big money deal was done. Gregory, not the quietest of men, said at the time that he could have shot Dwight for wanting to leave Villa! However, this was only an indication of the high regard he had for Dwight and showed how sad he was at losing such a great player.

Yorkey's United career began with a bang, scoring twice on his home debut versus Charlton and then bagging another a few days later at Coventry. The doubters in the United crowd were soon to be silenced as Dwight went from strength to strength, scoring "for fun" in both the Premier League and the Champion's League. He scored in the games with Bayern Munich, Brondby, Juventus and Barcelona, as

well as grabbing a brace of headers from David Beckham crosses against Inter Milan at Old Trafford, proving that he is capable of unlocking any defence in world football.

In addition to his almost telepathic understanding with Andy Cole, the service Dwight Yorke receives from David Beckham, Ryan Giggs and Paul Scholes means that United look likely to score whenever they're in the opposition's half. The 29 goals he scored in United's Treble winning season, Dwight's first at Old Trafford, and 23 goals in 1999/2000, is the sort of return only the most optimistic manager could have dreamt of. Yorke grabbed thirteen goals up to and including the equaliser against Necaxa in the FIFA World Club Championship during 1999/2000 which included braces against Leeds, Southampton and West Ham. This was followed by almost two months without a goal when he was in and out of the side, but he came back with a bang, answering his critics by grabbing a superb hat-trick in the 3-1 win over Derby on 11 March 2000 at Old Trafford. From then on he went from strength to strength, scoring against Fiorentina in the Champion's League, Leicester in the Premiership and twice in the 4-0 defeat of Bradford City at Valley Parade. In just a fortnight at the end of March, Yorkey had bagged a total of seven goals. He also displayed great goalscoring instincts with his two strikes against Chelsea in United's 3-2 victory in April, the first of which was bizarre – Dwight's tenacity was rewarded as he charged down Ed de Goey's clearance, the ball ricocheting into the net. The second was a true goal poacher's effort which won the match for United.

However, it is not just Dwight's goalscoring prowess that has earnt him rave reviews — his all round play has brought a new dimension to United's attack. He has partnered Andy Cole, Teddy Sheringham and Ole Gunnar Solskjaer up front and looked comfortable with all three — opposition defences just don't know what to do!

DWIGHT YORKE

Full Name: Dwight Eversley Yorke
Position: Forward
Nickname(s): Yorkey
Date of Birth: 3 November 1971
Place of Birth: Canaan, Trinidad & Tobago
Height: 5'11"
Weight: 12st. 7lb.
Previous Clubs: Signal Hill, St Clairs, Aston Villa
United Debut: vs West Ham
at Upton Park 22/8/98 (Premier League)
First United Goal: vs Charlton
at Old Trafford 7/9/98 (Premier League)
Total United Appearances: 89 (+ 9 as sub)
Total United Goals: 52

SOLID AS A ROCK

The emergence of Jaap Stam as one of the most powerful central defenders in world football may well prove to be Fergie's best bit of transfer business yet!

Like Dwight Yorke, Jaap Stam arrived at Old Trafford with an enormous price tag (£10.5 million – at the time United's record transfer and the biggest sum ever paid for a defender) and he had something to prove. He had been recognised as Dutch Player of the Year the previous season and had helped Holland to the Semi Finals of the World Cup in the summer, but the majority of journalists in this country felt that Stam would find it difficult in the ultra competitive Premier League. His early performances suggested that they could be right, as he struggled to come to terms with the pace of the English game.

Stam had a reputation in Holland as something of a slow starter. He'd still been playing outside the Dutch first division for Cambur Leeuwarden as late as 1994 but it was only a matter of time before he started to stamp his authority on United's matches. His increasingly assured performances, particularly in United's 2-0 victory over Liverpool at Old Trafford had critics eating their words. At the start of 1999 as United made their charge towards the Treble, Stam finally moved into top gear, pulling together the United defence into a solid, virtually impenetrable unit in front of Peter Schmeichel in his last year at the club. Having lost 3-2 at Old Trafford to Middlesbrough in December, United didn't lose for the rest of the season — another 33 games! It was the outstanding form of Jaap Stam that was mostly responsible for this remarkable run.

Stam was rock solid in the San Siro against Inter Milan in the Champion's League Quarter Final, so much so, that Ronaldo was substituted after an ineffectual first half. He also held the whole defence together in the FA Cup Semi Final Replay with Arsenal as United's 10 men held out against the rampant Gunners during extra time. This allowed Ryan Giggs to score one of the greatest goals of all time to keep the Treble dream alive. When Jaap Stam held the European Cup aloft on that magical night in Barcelona he'd answered his critics: in his first season at Old Trafford he'd won the Premier League, FA Cup and Champion's League — some slow starter!

Stam's second season for United began the same way as his first, with defeat in the Charity Shield by Arsenal, then an uncharacteristic blunder saw Nick Barmby's header deflect off him into his own net to gift Everton a point in the first Premier League game of the year. However, Stam once more worked his way out of a spot of poor form and as the games went by, he grew in confidence and stature. Fine performances in the Champion's League away at Marseille and Croatia Zagreb were followed by equally impressive displays in the Premier League, as Stam and Roy Keane presented an almost solid obstacle through the middle. Fantastic saving tackles, like the one on Benito Carbone of Aston Villa at Old Trafford, and blocked shots, such as Faustino Asprilla's blocked effort in United's 1-0 World Club Cup victory over Palmeiras, have seen Stam become recognised as one of the greatest defenders in world football. Adjectives like reliable, dependable and colossal are now regularly attributed to Stam in the media and his name must be one of the first on Sir Alex Ferguson's team-sheet every week. The impressive thing is that Stam is still only 27 ... his best is probably yet to come! ●

JAAP STAM

Full Name: Jakob Stam
Position: Central Defender
Date of Birth: 17 July 1972
Place of Birth: Kampen, Holland
Height: 6'3"
Weight: 13st. 9lb.
Previous Clubs: PEC Zwolle, Cambur Leeuwarden, Willem II, PSV Eindhoven
United Debut: vs Arsenal at Wembley 9/8/98 (Charity Shield)
1st United Goal: vs Leicester at Filbert Street 16/1/99 (Premier League)
Total United Appearances: 101 (+1 as sub)
Total United Goals: 1

FRED THE RED IN..
FRED'S SPECIAL DAY!

FLIXPIX

SIR ALEX PUTS FRED AND THE TEAM THROUGH THEIR PACES...
FRED GETS NUT-MEGGED BY YORKEY...
HE SHOOTS WIDE FROM SIX YARDS,...
AND FALLS OVER THE BALL...
vodafone

AFTER TRAINING...
FRED, YOU WERE VERY DISAPPOINTING TODAY. DON'T WORRY, THOUGH - EVERYONE HAS AN OFF DAY. BEFORE YOU GET CHANGED, CAN YOU GET MY TRACKSUIT TOP FOR ME - IT'S OVER BY THE GOAL.
GLOOM

I CAN'T BELIEVE THAT EVERYONE'S FORGOTTEN MY BIRTHDAY........

PUFF PANT
DRESSING ROOM

vodafone
SURPRISE SURPRISE!!

MANY HAPPY RETURNS!!
HAPPY BIRTHDAY!!

Fred
YOU DIDN'T THINK WE'D REALLY FORGOTTEN IT WAS YOUR BIRTHDAY TODAY, DID YOU FRED?

THANKYOU EVERYONE! THIS IS MY BEST!!! BIRTHDAY EVER!!!

MIDFIELD DYNAMO

Paul Scholes has often been referred to as the "unsung hero" in the United squad, but his impressive goalscoring record and heroics for England have proven his worth beyond any doubt

Paul Scholes was born in Salford and joined United in 1991 as a trainee, signing professional forms just two years later. He helped United win the 1992 FA Youth Cup and he exploded into the First Team at Portman Road, Ipswich, in September 1994 with two goals in a 3-2 victory. At this early stage of his career, Paul played in a striking role and his qualities as a finisher pushed him into regular First Team contention although he only started six games in the 1994-95 season. He also made 11 appearances as a sub and finished that campaign with five goals. With Eric Cantona's long suspension the following year, a space was created in the middle of United's midfield and Paul responded magnificently with outstanding performances, scoring 14 goals.

In the 1997-98 season Sir Alex Ferguson partnered Scholes with Roy Keane in the heart of midfield. Once there, Paul showed that he could not only score goals from midfield with the regularity of United "great" Bryan Robson, but he was also prepared to battle for every ball and harry opponents at every opportunity. Coupled with the tenacity and strength of Keane, this partnership regularly kept the impressive Nicky Butt on the bench, although when Keane's injuries led to a long term absence, Scholes and Butt were thrown together in the centre of United's midfield. It was during this period that Scholes' ability shone through, so much so that he came to the attention of the then England Manager, Glenn Hoddle who picked him for England's France 98 World Cup squad. Paul responded by appearing in every game of the tournament and scoring in the opening game against Tunisia with a spectacular 20 yard shot.

On his return from France, Paul started where he left off the previous year with battling performances and important goals, including a late equaliser against Inter Milan in the San Siro Stadium. The 1998-99 season was truly remarkable for both United and Paul Scholes – as United claimed the Treble, Scholes carved a niche for himself as the premier attacking midfielder in the country. Overall however, the year was a pretty mixed one for Paul — he scored an international hat-trick at Wembley as England beat Poland 3-1 and he netted the second goal in United's 2-0 FA Cup Final win over Newcastle, but he was sent off for England in a 0-0 draw with Sweden and became the first English player ever to get his marching orders at Wembley. He also missed the European Cup Final itself through suspension after being booked in Turin against Juventus in the Semi-Final.

The 1999/2000 season began superbly for Scholes, both for United and England. He scored goals against Sheffield Wednesday, Coventry (after coming on as a 61st minute sub and turning the game United's way) and Aston Villa in the Premiership. He also scored against Marseille and Valencia in the Champion's League and grabbed his two predatory goals for England at Hampden Park in the Euro 2000 Play-Off versus Scotland, ensuring a place in the Finals for England. However, he had been dogged by a niggling hernia problem all season and this saw him miss out on Manchester United's Brazilian adventure in FIFA's World Club Championships. Is it a coincidence that United's relatively poor performance in this tournament came in the absence of their ginger-haired midfield dynamo?

Once back in the First Team, however, Scholes was soon back to his formidable best, scoring a magnificent volleyed goal from the edge of the box at Bradford, and grabbing his first ever United hat-trick in the 7-1 demolition of West Ham on 1 April. Older England fans have likened Scholes to World Cup winner and flame-haired battler Alan Ball and it would be no surprise if, by the end of his career, Paul Scholes also had a World Cup Winners medal alongside the many accolades he has already won with United. ●

PAUL SCHOLES

Full Name: Paul Scholes
Position: Midfield
Born: 16 November 1974, Salford
Height: 5'7"
Weight: 11st. 8lb.
Previous Clubs: None
United Debut: vs Ipswich Town 24/9/94
First United Goal: vs Ipswich Town 24/9/94
Total United Appearances: 165 (+61 as sub)
Total United goals: 60

WING WIZARD

The name Ryan Giggs is synonymous with the incredible success Manchester United has enjoyed over the last ten years. He was one of the first of "Fergie's Fledglings" to find his feet in the United First Team and his rise to worldwide fame must surely have inspired those that followed like Beckham, Butt, Scholes and the Neville brothers. In 1987 Giggs signed as a schoolboy for Manchester United, despite having attended Manchester City's School of Excellence, and turned professional on 29 November 1990. His League debut came barely three months later, but on 4 May he thrilled the Old Trafford crowd with the only goal in the Manchester derby. A star was born!

The next season saw Giggs start 38 games and win his first trophy, the Rumbelows Cup (League Cup) after a 1-0 Wembley win over Nottingham Forest. The media dubbed him "the new George Best" as he became a First Team regular in 1992, and his dazzling wing play and memorable goals helped United claim their first League title in 26 years. The next year Giggs scored 13 goals which helped United claim the FA Cup and League double. The following season was hampered by injury and when Sir Alex Ferguson decided the time was right to play the youngsters in 1995/96, Giggs was one of the more experienced members of the team at the grand old age of 22! He didn't disappoint in his new responsibility, playing with a maturity and level-headedness far beyond his years, helping United to bag another FA Cup and League double.

Europe was the next big challenge for United. When they met the strong Portuguese side FC Porto in 1997's Quarter Final they trounced them 4-0, with Giggs the main destroyer playing through the centre of midfield. United lost in the Semi Final to Borussia Dortmund, but it was clear that this United team, with the prompting of Giggs, offered United their best hope of European glory

It is hard to believe that Ryan Giggs is stil only 27 – he seems to have been producing world class performances for United for years

for many years. 1997/98 was ultimately unsuccessful fo both United and Giggs as Arsenal grabbed the double, the European Cup drifted away and a persistent hamstring injury prevented Giggs from having much impact on the vital run in He did score a memorable solo goal against Juventus in the Champion's League, prompting Juventus Coach Marcello Lippi to say: 'Giggs is a truly superb player.'

The summer of 1998 saw Ryan shake off any lingering injury worries and he began the Treble season with renewed vigour, scoring four goals in as many Champion's League games. His superb form up until Christmas 1998 was threatened by more hamstring troubles and a fractured foot but Giggs returned earlier than expected and was soon back on top form. With United down to 10 men in extra time in the replay of the FA Cup semi-final against Arsenal, Giggs pounced on a loose pass from Patrik Vieira inside his own half, raced through the heart of the Arsenal defence, beating four players, and blasted an unstoppable shot past David Seaman from an acute angle. The tightest defence in Europe and one of the world's best goalkeepers had been undone in style. The Treble soon followed and there is no doubt tha Ryan was one of the main architects of United's success.

Giggs missed the start of last season, but in the game with Sheffield Wednesday he was at his best, supplying devastating crosses for Paul Scholes to open the scoring after only 8 minutes and for the second goal from Dwight Yorke. Giggs left the field to a standing ovation from the United faithful. He also supplied the ammunition for Roy Keane's winner in the World Club Championship victory over Palmeiras and was awarded the Most Valuable Player Award (and a Toyota Celica!) More goals followed, including a brace at West Ham, although it has always been his subtle passing and pin-point crossing tha marks Giggs out from the crowd. His form in the new year was nothing short of spectacular. The fact that United again finished the season as the Premier League's top scorers, breaking the Premier League scoring record in the process, is due in no small measure to the quality service from the Welsh Wing Wizard.

RYAN GIGGS

Full Name: Ryan Joseph Giggs
Position: Midfield
Born: 29 November 1973, Cardiff, Wales
Height: 5'11"
Weight: 10st. 10lb.
Previous Clubs: None
United Debut: vs Everton 2/3/91
First United Goal: vs Manchester City 4/5/94
United Appearances: 368 (+32 as sub)
Total United goals: 83

BROTHERS

As the first of the United 'young lions' to represent England, Gary Neville blazed a trail from the United Youth Team to the England squad for the likes of David Beckham, Paul Scholes, Nicky Butt and his younger brother Phil. One of the most reliable defenders in the country, Gary is a mature and tough-tackling right or centre back whose name is always one of the first on the team sheet at Old Trafford. Such is his reputation, that his two unfortunate errors against Vasco da Gama in the FIFA World Club Championships were greeted with shock back home.

Gary signed as a professional in January 1993, having already played for the First Team in Europe, appearing in the UEFA Cup against Torpedo Moscow in September 1992. At the time, Gary was part of United's successful Youth teams of 1992 and 1993. Making his league debut in the last game of the 1993/94 season, he broke into the United First Team the following year and by the end of that season, he was firmly in place on the right side of United's defence. The 1995/96 season was one to remember for Gary. It began in June with England's tour of the Far East where he made his England debut versus Japan. He went on to make 30 appearances for United, collecting a Premier League and FA Cup double, and was part of England's Euro 96 squad, playing in four games and only missing out on the Semi-final against Germany through suspension. That was quite a year for a player who was still only 21!

The next season saw Gary as consistent as ever with another 30 appearances to his name. He also got onto the score-sheet for the first time with an all important goal which helped earn a point against Middlesbrough ... and he collected another Premier League winner's medal! With Arsenal pipping United to the Double in 1997/98, Gary missed out on more silver-ware, but his 40 plus appearances for the First Team helped him to secure a place in England's squad for the 1998 World Cup. He was now a regular for both club and country. The Treble season began with upheaval in the United defence with the departure of Gary Pallister and the arrival of Jaap Stam. This wasn't helped by injuries to Henning Berg and Ronny Johnsen and although Gary often found himself partnering Stam in the centre of defence rather than out on the right, his level of performance never suffered. In fact, Gary's versatility and calm under pressure helped Stam and the United back line settle down in time to begin their fantastic unbeaten run in 1999 which took them to ultimate triumph in Barcelona. Gary also managed to double his United goal tally with the winner at Old Trafford versus Everton.

The 1999/2000 season started frustratingly for Gary as a groin injury sidelined him until late August and the European Super Cup match with Lazio. Gary then went on to miss a further two months with more groin problems but returned against Strum Graz in the Champion's League. The away match at Derby in November provided evidence of another aspect of Gary's game which has improved over the years, his setting-up of chances for his attacking colleagues. It was his cross which enabled Nicky Butt to open the scoring in a 2-1 victory. A similar cross and weak clearance allowed Roy Keane to open the scoring in the Champion's League game with Valencia in December.

With opposition defences desperate to prevent David Beckham from whipping in his trademark crosses, Gary's support on the right hand side and ever-improving delivery into the penalty area have added yet another dimension to the United attack. But it is in defence that Gary's strengths lie and his consistently good performances at the back have helped lay the foundations for another successful season at United.

GARY NEVILLE

Full Name: Gary Alexander Neville
Position: Defender
Born: 18 February 1975, Bury, England
Height: 5'10"
Weight: 11st. 7lb.
Previous Clubs: None
United Debut: vs Torpedo Moscow 16/9/92
First United Goal: vs Middlesbrough 5/5/97
United Appearances: 238 (+11 as sub)
Total United goals: 2

GARY

IN ARMS

Two years younger than his brother Gary, Phil Neville has followed him from Youth Team glories to the England squad. However, he is a different player to his brother and has not so easily claimed a United First Team spot as his own. This is not due to any deficiencies, rather the excellent form of Denis Irwin at left back, Phil's natural position. However, Phil's fantastic versatility has enabled Sir Alex Ferguson to use him as back-up for all the defensive positions as well as in the midfield and, on occasions, on the left wing as well! His ferocious tackling, superb pace and excellent vision mark him out as one of United's finest players ... in any position!

Phil Neville captained the United Youth Team to success in the 1995 Youth Cup Final. That same season he made his First Team debut against Wrexham in a 5-1 FA Cup victory, all this just a year after he signed professional terms at Old Trafford! It was in the 1995/96 season when Alan Hansen made his famous "you can't win anything with kids" comment, that Phil joined his brother regularly in the First Team squad and although his opportunities were limited he still made 24 appearances that year. In fact, he actually played in the 1-0 FA Cup Final victory over Liverpool instead of his brother and soon afterwards, he was capped by England aged only 19. He finished the season with an England cap and Premier League and FA Cup winner's medals.

The following year was not quite so good for Phil as an ankle injury and then glandular fever robbed him of most of the season. When he was back to full fitness at the start of 1997/98 he found himself covering for a host of midfield injuries as Sir Alex Ferguson used his squad resources to the full. Phil also opened his United goalscoring account with the winner at Stamford Bridge against Chelsea in the Premier League encounter. Although he never disappointed, his lack of a settled First Team place cost him dear as he was heartbreakingly omitted from the 22-man England squad for the World Cup in France.

Phil's second United goal came in the November of United's Treble-winning season when he scored one of United's five against Brondby in the Champion's League tie at Old Trafford. Early on in the 1998/99 season, Phil often played in defence alongside his brother as the new United back line took time to gel. Later on in the season, he was moved to a position on the left side of midfield. However, he was often on the substitutes bench, ready to deputise in case of injury or tactical change. In fact, he made 28 starts and was thrown on as sub a further nine times that year. His contribution to United's Treble success cannot be underestimated.

The 1999/2000 season began with Phil playing mostly at right-back in place of his brother, and his form was outstanding. His crosses set up Dwight Yorke's goal against Leeds and Andy Cole's superb bicycle kick effort against Leicester came after Ole Gunnar Solskjaer had flicked on Phil's centre. He often found himself fulfilling midfield roles, such as in the game at Old Trafford against Wimbledon, and another aspect of his superb all-round game was his use as a man-marker on Gianfranco Zola of Chelsea. However, once again Phil spent a lot of his time on the bench and throughout the year the triple substitution of Phil Neville, Ole Gunnar Solskjaer and Teddy Sheringham was often used as United chased games in the closing stages. In the future, Phil Neville may well slot into a left back position when Denis Irwin's outstanding career comes to an end, but in the meantime, he is more than happy to serve Manchester United in whatever capacity is necessary.

PHIL NEVILLE

Full Name: Philip John Neville
Position: Defender
Born: 21 January 1977, Bury, England
Height: 5'11"
Weight: 11st. 11lb.
Previous Clubs: None
United Debut: vs Wrexham 28/1/95
First United Goal: vs Chelsea 28/2/98
United Appearances: 148 (+42 as sub)
Total United goals: 2

UNITED crossword

Fill in the answers to this United crossword and then rearrange the letters in the shaded boxes to reveal what United were known as before they became Manchester United.

ACROSS

3 Who were the two joint hosts of Euro 2000? Holland and ___________ (7)
4 Which team ended United's involvement in 1999/2000's Worthington Cup? (5,5)
5 In which Italian city do Internazionale play their football? (5)
7 How many goals did Dwight Yorke score against Derby in the Premier League on 11 March 2000? (5)
11 Where do United's Manchester rivals City play their home games? (5,4)
13 In which Spanish city did United lift the Champion's League trophy in 1999? (9)
15 In what part of Manchester is United's Premier League Academy? (10)
17 What is Sir Alex Ferguson's nickname? (6)
18 How many goals did United score against Nottingham Forest in the Premier League in Feb 1999? (5)
19 At the end of a game, if United have scored 3 goals and the opposition only 1, what have we done? (3)
22 In what position does Denis Irwin play? Left ________ (4)
23 Which Italian team did Gabriel Batistuta play for in the 1999/2000 Champion's League? (10)
25 For which Premier League team does Nick Barmby play? (7)
26 Which Premier League team's nickname is The Black Cats? (9)

DOWN

1 Name the famous Frenchman nicknamed "Le God"? Eric _________ (7)
2 What is the first name of David Beckham's wife? _________ (8)
3 What is the name of the West Indian cricketer who is one of Dwight Yorke's best friends? (5,4)
6 Which company sponsors the English League Cup? (11)
8 Which United player was born in California? Paul _________ (8)
9 Where was the first ever FIFA World Club Championships held? (6)
10 How many times have United won the FA Cup? (3)
12 In which country would you find Galatasary? (6)
14 To which Italian club did Massimo Taibi go on loan in early 2000? (6)
16 & 20 To which club did United pay £7 million for Andy Cole? (9,6)
21 What is Phil Neville's middle name? (4)
23 How many Premier League Championships did United win in the 1990s? (4)
24 Against which team was David Beckham sent off in the FIFA World Club Championships? (6)

FAST FACT

On 18 November 1995 Ryan Giggs scored after just 16 seconds in the Premier League game with Southampton – this is the fastest ever goal in United's history!

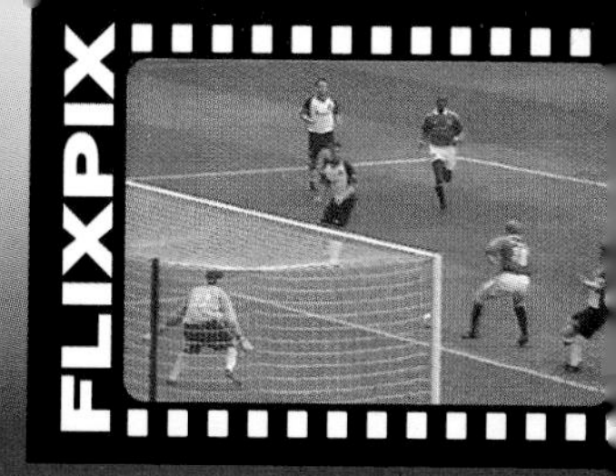

CHECK PAGE 64 FOR THE ANSWERS!

1999-2000 SEASON REVIEW

With the Treble in the bag, the 1999/2000 season began with exciting challenges for Sir Alex Ferguson and his team. Could they become the first English team to retain the European Cup since Nottingham Forest in 1980? Could they win the Premier League for the sixth time in just eight years and could they become the first ever FIFA World Club Champions? Let's see how it turned out ...

AUGUST

The 1999/2000 season began in the same way as the Treble campaign, with defeat in the pre-season curtain-raiser The Charity Shield at Wembley. Arsenal ended **United's** incredible 33 game unbeaten run, which had lasted for the whole of 1999, by winning 2-1. A Kanu penalty and Ray Parlour's shot on the run cancelled out David Beckham's rasping 30-yard free kick in the first half. The first Premier League fixture sent **United** to Merseyside to face Walter Smith's Everton side. Here, **Manchester United** saw the shape of things to come as dogged resistance from a packed Everton defence looked to contain the Champions rather than beat them. For much of the season, both home and away, it seemed that **United** would face teams sitting back and hoping to hit on the break, looking for just a point against the Treble winners. Following some crisp interplay between Ole Gunnar Solskjaer and Andy Cole, Dwight Yorke opened **United's** Premiership account with a clinical finish past Paul Gerard. But although **United** were running the game at their own pace, Everton had their own chances and as the game drew to a close, Nick Barmby's far post header was deflected into his own net by Jaap Stam past a nervous Mark Bosnich to clinch a 1-1 draw. **United's** territorial superiority had not turned into a win and Sir Alex Ferguson must have been disappointed with the start of the Premier League marathon.

United's first League game at Old Trafford was much more like it, as Sheffield Wednesday were put to the sword. Quality strikes from Paul Scholes and Dwight Yorke before half time and second-half goals from Cole and Solskjaer completed a comprehensive 4-0 victory. Leeds United visited Old Trafford three days later for a much tighter clash. Leeds dominated much of a goalless first half and if Harry Kewell's 66th minute effort had not hit the inside of the post, the result may have been different. As it was, Yorke pounced twice within three minutes in the last fifteen minutes to claim the points. Leading

up to the clash with Arsenal at Highbury, the newspapers were full of Roy Keane's impending contract negotiations, which would make him the highest paid player in the Premiership, and it was this game probably more than any other which served to highlight the Irishman's vital importance to the cause.

The pace throughout the first half was relentless and Arsenal took a 1-0 advantage into half time after Freddie Ljungberg's well-taken goal on 41 minutes. The second half was equally passionate and exciting and after an hour Roy Keane stamped his authority on the game by equalising following a one-two with Cole on the edge of the Arsenal penalty box. Keane continued to control the centre and, as the temperature rose, a confrontation between him and Patrick Vieira resulted in an ugly mêlée involving nearly all the players on the pitch. Keane remained cool and with just two minutes left he followed up on Ryan Giggs' blocked shot to slide the ball under Manninger to win the game 2-1 for **United.** An away trip to Coventry followed, as did three more Premiership points as Paul Scholes came off the bench to grab the first and Yorke headed home the second from a Beckham cross. **United** followed a disappointing 1-0 reverse against Lazio in the European Super Cup held in Monaco, with ex-**United** target Marcelo Salas grabbing the only goal, with a hugely impressive 5-1 home victory over Newcastle United. The Magpies arrived at Old Trafford managerless after the departure of Ruud Gullit and Andy Cole showed no sympathy for his former employers by scoring no less than four times, Giggs getting the other, after Dabizas had been sent off.

SEPTEMBER

September began with a trip to Anfield, the home of Liverpool. This was one of those blood and thunder games that makes the English Premier League famous. **United** went into the game with a long injury list which included Keane, Irwin and Gary Neville. Their first-half performance was brilliant and such was the pressure on the Liverpool defence that Jamie Carragher was forced into conceding two own goals. Andy Cole made it 3-0 and it looked as though that was that. However, Sami Hyypiä's first Liverpool goal and Patrik Berger's fine finish ensured a dramatic conclusion to the game, especially after Cole was sent off for lashing out at Rigobert Song. **United** held on to a good 3-2 victory which extended their unbeaten league sequence to 27 games. The first Champion's League fixture of the season followed, with Croatia Zagreb visiting Old Trafford. With the injury crisis at **United** deepening, the team's performance was disappointing and the game ended in a drab 0-0 draw. Wimbledon came to Old Trafford next and looked to be going home with all the points after Walid Badir's crisp finish on 16 minutes. With Ryan Giggs limping off and the team huffing and puffing without much reward, it looked as if **United's** proud unbeaten record would disappear until Jordi Cruyff emerged from the shadows to bag an equaliser with just 15 minutes left. **United** won their next game in the Champion's League, away at Sturm Graz, with goals from Keane, Yorke and Cole in the first half, although Raimond Van der Gouw saved Vastic's penalty in the second half and the Austrians missed several opportunities to put pressure on the **United** defence.

Low on confidence, Southampton arrived at Old Trafford and although **United** were not at their best, they were controlling the game at 2-1 early in the second half with goals from Sheringham and Yorke replying to Marian Pahars' opener for the Saints. Then Matthew Le Tissier hit a hopeful shot from 25 yards which rolled slowly towards and then unbelievably past the embarrassed goalkeeper Massimo Taibi. Dwight Yorke put **United** back in front, but with 16 minutes to go Le Tissier grabbed his second to earn Southampton an unlikely point. The last game of September was the home Champion's League tie versus Marseille and for most of the match it looked as though the French side would emerge victorious after Ibrahim

BELOW (left to right): Paul Scholes takes on Silvinho in the Charity Shield; Dwight Yorke is congratulated after opening United's Premier League account at Everton; Leeds' Darren Huckerby comes up against Jaap Stam; Becks fires a free kick through the Arsenal wall in the 2-1 victory at Highbury; Andy Cole jumps with Liverpool's Rigobert Song while Dominic Matteo looks on; Teddy Sheringham slides in on Jason Euell.

Bakayoko's 41st minute goal. However, like in the Nou Camp the previous May, **United** left it late and with strikes from Cole after 78 minutes and Scholes after 82 minutes, the points were safe.

OCTOBER

October began in disastrous fashion with **United's** heaviest defeat in three years inflicted by a rampant Chelsea in the autumn sunshine at Stamford Bridge. First half goals from Gustavo Poyet and Chris Sutton were followed by the sending off of Nicky Butt for a petulant flick at Dennis Wise. Although Jaap Stam strove manfully to hold the defence together in the second period, further goals from Poyet, and Jody Morris and a Henning Berg own goal rubbed salt into the **United** wounds. Fortunately, there followed an international break which meant that the next competitive fixture was away at Aston Villa in the Worthington Cup 10 days later. Fergie sent out a reserve team at Villa Park so it was no real surprise that Villa cruised into the next round with a 3-0 victory, the goals from Julian Joachim, Ian Taylor and Steve Stone. Back in the Premiership, **United** returned to winning ways as they despatched the hapless Watford with a commanding display which saw goals from Yorke, Cole (2) and Irwin. Alex Ferguson was nearly able to field a full-strength team and the gulf in class was evident as **United** bossed the game from start to finish.

Following heavy downpours in the South of France, **United**'s Champion's League fixture with Marseille had looked in doubt right up until the kick-off, although once the game got going it was the French team who adapted to the boggy conditions best. Marseille won the game with a 69th minute strike from William Gallas and so ended **Manchester United's** long unbeaten Champion's League run. In London for the Premiership clash with Tottenham Hotspur, **United** looked to end their recent run of poor results away from home. But it was not to be as George Graham's North London outfit took all three points with goals from Steffen Iversen, an unfortunate Paul Scholes own goal and a 35-yard thunderbolt from right-back Stephen Carr, despite going behind to Ryan Giggs' smartly finished opener. **United** eventually got a result on their travels with a convincing 2-1 victory over Croatia Zagreb in the Champion's League. In a game that the Champions utterly dominated, Keane's second-half deflected shot put the game beyond doubt after another superb David Beckham free kick goal had made it 1-0 at half time. Despite Prosinecki's late consolation, **United** were safely through to the second phase of the competition and as Ferguson rested some of his stars, he could reflect on a job well done. October ended with a crushing 3-0 defeat of Aston Villa at Old Trafford. With David Beckham producing possibly his best form of the season to date, Scholes, Cole and Keane clinically finished moves which all emanated from the right foot of the England midfielder. **United** seemed to be coming into form as autumn turned to winter.

NOVEMBER

Manchester United brushed aside a spirited Sturm Graz side to top the Champion's League Group D with goals from Solskjaer and Keane. Although the performance was more workmanlike than exhilarating, Sir Alex Ferguson must have been pleased as some of his fringe players had been drafted in to replace regulars who were out through suspension or injury. The game was won after the late introduction of Phil Neville and, although Sturm Graz scored from a late penalty, **United** were home and dry. Two Premiership matches followed; home against Leicester City and away at Derby. After these two fairly comfortable victories, **United** were top of the League and they still hadn't moved into top gear. Two quality goals from Andy Cole, one a stunning bicycle kick, defeated Martin O'Neill's Leicester side despite some solid resistance. Cole was on the mark again at Derby's Pride Park a fortnight later, having spent the two intervening "Battle of Britain" play-off encounters with Scotland on the England bench. Nicky Butt, returning to the side after a hernia operation, bagged **United's** first goal in a bad-tempered match which saw Derby's Stefan Schnoor sent off.

The Second Phase of the Champion's League began with a disastrous night in Florence as Gabriel Batistuta and Rui Costa ran the **United** defence ragged with some inspired play. An uncharacteristically sloppy backpass from Roy Keane allowed "El Batigol" to score Fiorentina's first, and then Batistuta's

FLIXPIX

LEFT (from left): Jaap Stam uses his head at Chelsea; Coley finds a way through the Spurs defence; Gary Neville congratulates Nicky Butt after his goal at Derby; United collect the World Club Cup; West Ham's Steve Lomas takes hold of Dwight Yorke

persistence in harrying Henning Berg into a mistake on the left side of defence enabled Balbo to wrap up the game at 2-0. On 30 November, **United** played out the World Club Cup against South American Champions Palmeiras of Brazil in Tokyo. Although the fanatical Japanese crowd were cheering on David Beckham, it was Ryan Giggs' moment of magic which allowed Roy Keane to score the only goal. This win saw **United** collect the Toyota Cup, becoming the first British side ever to win this contest between the European and South American Champions!

DECEMBER

Fergie allowed himself the luxury of resting Beckham, Yorke and Cole for Everton's visit to Old Trafford and played the "baby-faced assassin" Ole Gunnar Solskjaer up front for a rare start. After 25 minutes, **United** were 1-0 down after Francis Jeffers' tap-in, and had lost Mark Bosnich to injury. However, Denis Irwin banged home a penalty after Richard Dunne had handled and from then on, it was the Ole Gunnar Solskjaer show as the Norwegian bagged four goals for the second time in 1999. In truth, once **United** went 2-1 up, there was no contest. Some of the play was outstanding, especially from Ryan Giggs who tormented an already dispirited Everton defence throughout the second half.

Before the start of the Champion's League game with Valencia, Roy Keane signed a new contract with the club to end months of press speculation and in true "Roy of the Rovers" style he scored a superb opening goal. Here was a **United** team back to its very best European form and Valencia, despite having the lively Lopez up front, were simply no match for the Champions. Solskjaer and Scholes scored the second and third goals but by the end, the 3-0 scoreline simply didn't do the performance justice. Back on form and with the Champion's League on hold until February, **United** focused on consolidating their position at the top of the Premier League. This they did by scoring 4 goals in consecutive matches. Firstly they defeated West Ham United 4-2 in a truly fantastic match. The Hammers set out to fight fire with fire, producing an engrossing spectacle. With Beckham and Giggs firing on all cylinders, **United** were simply unstoppable down the flanks and West Ham had no answer to Dwight Yorke and the tireless Paul Scholes in the middle. Both Giggs and Yorke scored two goals while West Ham replied with a brace from the extrovert Paulo di Canio. It was much more "one way traffic" at Old Trafford in the next game as Bradford tried to rein in the rampant Champions. In all fairness, the Bantams, although up against severe pressure, had managed to hold out for 75 minutes, but when Quinton Fortune scored his first **United** goal, the floodgates opened. Four minutes later Yorke scored **United's** second and with time running out Andy Cole and Roy Keane hit the net to make the scoreline 4-0 at the final whistle. **United's** final game of a memorable 1999 came at Sunderland's magnificent Stadium of Light and things could not have got off to a worse start as the home side raced into an early 2-0 lead through Gavin McCann and Niall Quinn. Keane pulled one back halfway through the first half, but for much of the game the Premiership new boys matched **United** and were unlucky not to hold on for the win. In the end, the Champions' quality proved too much for Sunderland and Nicky Butt's finish from the edge of the box after 86 minutes ensured that the points were shared.

JANUARY

The first two weeks of the new millennium saw **United** in South America competing for the first ever FIFA World Club Championships. Overall, the tournament was a disappointment with a 1-1 draw against Mexican side Necaxa, including David Beckham's dismissal, followed by a disastrous 3-1 defeat at the hands of Brazilian giants Vasco da Gama. The final game saw **United** beat Australians South Melbourne 2-0 with the two goals and superb performance of Quinton Fortune among the only good things to come out of **United**'s two weeks in the sun. Back home in late January, Ferguson's team was plunged straight into the deep end with the mighty Arsenal arriving at Old Trafford, confident of inflicting **United's** first home defeat for over a year. The Gunners started well and dominated the opening periods of play, so it was no real surprise when Freddie Ljungberg slapped a cross-shot into the far corner past Mark Bosnich to open the scoring. Alex Ferguson turned to his trusty substitute Teddy Sheringham as the game wore on and it looked as though the Arsenal rearguard would remain unbeaten. Just seven minutes after coming on, Teddy tapped home Beckham's centre to earn **United** a point and keep them in second spot, three points behind Leeds with two games in hand. One of those games followed quickly and a late David Beckham goal and a fantastic penalty save from Mark Bosnich were enough to beat Middlesbrough at Old Trafford and put **United** on top of the Premier League on goal difference.

FEBRUARY

February saw **United** play five Premiership matches and Sir Alex Ferguson and his team sought to strengthen their Premiership lead. They began with a 1-0 victory over bottom of the table Sheffield Wednesday, thanks to a 73rd minute finish from Teddy Sheringham who ran onto a lovely throughball from Ryan Giggs. However, the performance was not of the highest quality, prompting the press to point the finger of blame at a post-Brazilian hangover. A record Premier League crowd of 61,380 packed into Old Trafford to see **United** play Coventry. They were rewarded with a returning Andy Cole scoring one of the goals of the season, a delightful chip over the retreating Magnus Hedman. Cole went on to score a second from Becks' free kick and when Paul Scholes made it 3-1 with just fifteen minutes to go, everyone assumed the game was all over. However, Cedric Roussel scored his and Coventry's second just before the end to raise a few heart rates but when the final whistle was blown, **United** were six points clear at the top. Newcastle United's two goals by Alan Shearer and one by Scottish giant Duncan Ferguson saw **Manchester United** defeated for only the third time in the Premier League all season. The Magpies were a totally different team to the one beaten 5-1 at Old Trafford in August. **United** started well and should have been ahead before big Dunc struck on 26 minutes. There was a lot of frustration for **United**, especially when what looked like a blatant penalty was turned down; this boiled over when Roy Keane was dismissed for a second bookable offence just after the hour. From here there was no way back and Shearer's two late goals made the final score 3-0.

With Leeds now only three points behind **United** in the table, the game with the Yorkshire club at Elland Road was seen by many as an early Championship decider. That it was played with the passion and intensity deserving of such an occasion there is no doubt, but whether the 1-0 victory, with Cole getting the goal, would ultimately bring the title back to Old Trafford was not decided in this game. Apart from good efforts from Ian Harte and a missed sitter from Lee Bowyer, **United** were in complete control for most of the match and it was only in the last frantic minutes that Leeds looked likely to break their duck and salvage a point. The biggest talking point of the day was David Beckham's omission from the squad for this game, following an alleged training ground bust up with Alex Ferguson. February ended with a rather tame 2-2 draw with Wimbledon. The Dons took the lead through Euell after just two minutes only for Cruyff

THE FIRST FIFA WORLD CLUB CHAMPIONSHIPS

The biggest talking point in the football world at the start of the 1999/2000 season was whether **Manchester United** should participate in the FIFA World Championships to be held in Brazil in January 2000. Essentially, it was a no-win situation for **United** once FIFA had decided to hold the tournament in the middle of the English season and the tabloid media had a field day as the arrangements for the clubs withdrawal from the FA Cup were announced. At the time, there were many factors to be weighed up, not least the FA's insistence that England's chances of hosting the 2006 World Cup would be jeopardised if United didn't go. A lot of criticism was levelled at **United**, but it could be argued that the people who accused the club of treating the FA Cup with disdain were the same people who would have claimed that **United** didn't care about the good of the English game as a whole if they hadn't competed. The team eventually left for Brazil with the aim of becoming the Official World Champions, to add to the unofficial crown they already held after beating Palmeiras 1-0 in the World Club Cup. But it wasn't going to be easy. Playing three quality sides in just five days in intolerable heat after a few days of acclimatising was asking an awful lot of European players.

Ole Gunnar Solskjaer in action at the Maracana

United began the tournament against Necaxa of Mexico, who stunned them on 14 minutes when Cristian Montecinos scored direct from a free kick. However, the incident which filled the newspapers the next day occurred in the 42nd minute when David Beckham went in high on Salvador Cabrera. It was a challenge seen every day in the Premier League and may have warranted a caution, but referee Elizondo sent Beckham off, evoking memories of Becks' red card in France 98. Bosnich then saved Alex Aguinaga's 57th minute penalty and Yorke equalised two minutes from time to earn **United** a 1-1 draw.

United's Championships were effectively over after just 26 minutes of the next game with Vasco da Gama of Brazil when two defensive blunders from the normally reliable Gary Neville gifted two goals to Romario. Then a moment of genius from the enigmatic Edmundo put the game beyond **United** when he turned Mikael Silvestre and steered the ball passed Bosnich to put the Brazilians 3-0 up at half time. Nicky Butt scored a late consolation goal to make the final score 3-1. Now **United** were unable to reach the Final, so Sir Alex Ferguson gave his squad players a run-out against Australian's South Melbourne. Quinton Fortune took his chance in the First Team by grabbing a couple of well worked goals in the first 20 minutes. A large victory could have put **United** into the Third Place Play-off, but with the heat taking its toll, the game began to fizzle out and ended 2-0.

Corinthians of Brazil went on to be crowned the first Official World Club Champions after a poor final with Vasco da Gama finished goalless and went to penalties. Edmundo missed the decisive kick for Vasco da Gama and Corinthians won 4-3 in the shoot-out. **United** had already flown home by this time and probably the most important factor in Sir Alex Ferguson's mind was that his players had got through the tournament without injury.

to equalise with a crisp finish from Ryan Giggs' pass. Cort put Wimbledon back in front after an hour and **United** only managed to rescue a point after Giggs' superb skill down the left wing, reminiscent of the recently departed Sir Stanley Matthews, allowed Cole to shoot smartly past Neil Sullivan.

MARCH

With a resurgent Liverpool visiting Old Trafford in three days time, **United**'s first game in March, a Champion's League, Group B encounter with an out of form Bordeaux, allowed Fergie to rest Yorke and Scholes. Bordeaux started well, but it was not long before **United** stamped their authority on the game. The 2-0 victory was wrapped up without the team getting out of first gear. Giggs supplied the first goal on 42 minutes and it was his cross five minutes from time which allowed Sheringham to head home. Gérard Houllier's Liverpool came to Old Trafford in confident mood and grabbed the lead when Patrik Berger's vicious free kick beat Van Der Gouw. The points were shared when Solskjaer netted from another Giggs centre just before the interval while Liverpool's influential defender Sami Hyypiä was off the field receiving treatment on a knock inflicted, ironically, by Solskjaer. Chances came and went for both sides in the second half but the score remained 1-1 and Liverpool's 10-year wait for victory at Old Trafford continues.

The return match with Bordeaux was the next game and after just 9 minutes Van Der Gouw somehow allowed Michel Pavon's 30-yard shot to pass through his fingers into the net. Despite the sending off of Lilian Laslandes for his second yellow card after just 22 minutes and Roy Keane's equaliser after 33, **United** couldn't dominate the game and it wasn't until six minutes from time that Solskjaer, who had been on the pitch for just two minutes, grabbed all three points with a crisp finish past Ulrich Rame. Back in Premier League action against Derby, Dwight Yorke bagged his first league goal of the year 2000 in the 12th minute and went on to complete a fine hat-trick with two goals in three minutes halfway through the second half in a 3-1 victory. On 15 March Fiorentina came to Old Trafford in the Champion's League and **United** produced one of their best performances of the season, winning 3-1. **United** went behind after quarter of an hour to a wickedly swerving shot from Gabriel Batistuta before Andy Cole turned Tomas Repka on the edge of the box and rifled in a powerful right-foot shot to equalise. Keane put **United** in front on 32 minutes when he fired home the rebound after Henning Berg had headed against the bar. In the second period, Fiorentina's Rossitto was sent off and Yorke finished the scoring with twenty minutes left with a fine header to guarantee **United**'s place in the knockout stages. The biggest talking points from the next game were David Beckham's new shaven-headed hairstyle and his superb free kick which, together with Yorke's fifth goal in three games, condemned Leicester to a relatively straightforward 2-0 defeat.

United's last group game in the Champion's League took place in Valencia. With both teams happy with a point, it eventually fizzled out into a 0-0 draw although the Spanish side had started brightly initially looking for the 3-0 victory that would see them top the group. The last fixture in March saw **United** travel to relegation haunted Bradford and hand out a 4-0 thrashing with goals from Yorke (2), Scholes and Beckham. Scholes' effort was particularly memorable, a sensational volley from 20 yards direct from Becks' corner.

APRIL

United were not fooling around on the first day of April as they crushed West Ham 7-1 at Old Trafford with Paul Scholes scoring a fine hat-trick and Irwin, Cole, Beckham and Solskjaer also getting on the score-sheet despite going behind early on. It was some response to Hammers manager Harry Redknapp who had said before the match that **United** were not playing as well as last season! Three days later **United** travelled to Spain for the first leg of the Champion's League Quarter Final with Real Madrid. Mark Bosnich produced some great saves, most notably from Steve McManaman, to prevent Real scoring and although

BELOW (left to right): Dwight Yorke helps Teddy Sheringham celebrate his late equalising goal in the 1-1 draw with Arsenal; Andy Cole holds off Leeds' Lucas Radebe to score the only goal at Elland Road; Ole Gunnar Solskjaer challenges Derby's Matt Elliott during United's 3-1 victory at Old Trafford.

Dwight Yorke thought he had scored the vital away goal on 45 minutes it was ruled out for a dubious offside and the game ended 0-0. At Middlesbrough's Riverside Stadium on 10 April Andy Campbell scored for the home side after 18 minutes, while Giggs equalised just after the break. When Cole put **United** in front with an hour gone it seemed that **United** had got over their shaky start, especially as with 15 minutes to go, Scholes' piledriver made the score 3-1. Then Ince got one back for 'Boro. Quinton Fortune restored **United**'s two goal lead and with time running out Juninho pulled another goal back. In a thrilling finish **United** held on for a 4-3 victory. On 15 April Sunderland found themselves on the end of a 4-0 thrashing at Old Trafford as **United** broke the Premier League scoring record of 82 goals. Solskjaer scored twice, Nicky Butt netted following a Beckham centre and substitute Henning Berg scrambled home the fourth.

Real Madrid arrived at Old Trafford for the second leg of the Champion's League Quarter Final and proceeded to rain on **United**'s parade. With just 20 minutes gone Roy Keane diverted Michel Salgado's cross into his own net and Real had the away goal. At half time **United** were still in the contest, needing two goals to win the tie, however, after just seven minutes of the second period they trailed 3-0, two goals from Raul leaving **United** needing four goals. David Beckham scored a wondergoal after 64 minutes and Paul Scholes netted a late penalty, but there was no Nou Camp miracle this time and **United**'s Champion's League dreams were over for this season.

There were three Premier League games in the remainder of April and **United** scored three goals in each of them, wrapping up the title by half time of the first of them at Southampton with a free kick from David Beckham, a Francis Benali own goal and a clinical strike from Ole Gunnar Solskjaer. Goals from Yorke (2) and Solskjaer beat Chelsea at Old Trafford in the next game as **United**, on cruise control, emphasised how far they are ahead of the rest of the Premiership, stretching their lead to 16 points from second-placed Liverpool. The last match of a busy April was the away fixture at relegated Watford. This was a thrilling game which **United** won with Yorke, Giggs and substitute Cruyff netting the goals. However, Watford had led through Heidar Helguson before Micah Hyde and Nicky Butt were sent off on 64 minutes for a spot of "handbags". Tommy Mooney made the score 2-2 with 12 minutes remaining before Cruyff came off the bench to secure the 3-2 victory.

MAY

United's last home game of the season saw Tottenham Hotspur visit Old Trafford. Spurs had beaten **United** 3-1 back in October and this match produced the same scoreline although it was the team in red on top this time! With the Championship celebrations in full swing amongst the record 61,629 crowd, Solskjaer poked home from close range after 5 minutes before Chris Armstrong equalised with a fine diving header fifteen minutes later. Before half time the match was wrapped up as David Beckham scored his 50th **United** goal with a fine 20-yard strike and then Teddy Sheringham fired into the roof of the net against his former employers. When the final whistle blew, the **United** players were presented with the Premier League Trophy and soon after the champagne was flowing – see Pages 42 and 43! Sheringham was once again on the mark in **United**'s last game of the season against Aston Villa, scoring the only goal after 65 minutes when he steered the ball into the corner of the net after Jordi Cruyff's shot was blocked. This was a fairly tame match with Villa concentrating on their FA Cup Final appearance the following week and **United** missing eight First Team players.

So, the season ended with another win, another clean sheet and a total of 97 league goals. Sir Alex Ferguson and his team had collected their sixth Premier League title in eight years, but the big prize of the Champion's League had been snatched from their grasp by Real Madrid. The papers reported that a film entitled "Manchester United – The Movie" was being produced and in Monaco **Manchester United** were named "World Team of the Year" at the Laureus Sports Awards. Fabien Barthez arrived at Old Trafford for a world record fee for a goalkeeper while Ruud Van Nistelrooy's £19 million transfer broke down due to medical problems. As the players went on holiday or joined their national teams for Euro 2000, the start of the 2000/2001 season was only weeks away. Business as usual! ●

FINAL PREMIER LEAGUE TABLE

TEAM	P	W	D	L	GF	GA	PTS
MANCHESTER UNITED	38	28	7	3	97	45	91
ARSENAL	38	22	7	9	73	43	73
LEEDS UNITED	38	21	6	11	58	43	69
LIVERPOOL	38	19	10	9	51	30	67
CHELSEA	38	18	11	9	53	34	65
ASTON VILLA	38	15	13	10	46	35	58
SUNDERLAND	38	16	10	12	57	56	58
LEICESTER CITY	38	16	7	15	55	55	55
WEST HAM UNITED	38	15	10	13	52	53	55
TOTTENHAM HOTSPUR	38	15	8	15	57	49	53
NEWCASTLE UNITED	38	10	14	13	47	59	47
MIDDLESBROUGH	38	14	10	14	46	52	52
EVERTON	38	12	14	12	59	49	50
COVENTRY CITY	38	12	8	18	47	54	44
SOUTHAMPTON	38	12	8	18	45	62	44
DERBY COUNTY	38	9	11	18	44	57	38
BRADFORD CITY	38	9	9	20	38	68	36
WIMBLEDON	38	7	12	19	46	74	33
SHEFFIELD WEDNESDAY	38	8	7	23	38	70	31
WATFORD	38	6	6	26	35	77	24

CHAMPIONS LEAGUE STAGE 1 — GROUP D

TEAM	P	W	D	L	GF	GA	PTS
MANCHESTER UNITED	6	4	1	1	9	4	13
MARSEILLE	6	4	1	1	9	4	13
STURM GRAZ	6	4	1	1	9	4	13
CROATIA ZAGREB	6	4	1	1	9	4	13

CHAMPIONS LEAGUE STAGE 2 — GROUP B

TEAM	P	W	D	L	GF	GA	PTS
MANCHESTER UNITED	6	4	1	1	10	4	13
VALENCIA	6	3	1	2	9	5	10
FIORENTINA	6	2	2	2	7	8	8
BORDEAUX	6	0	2	4	5	14	2

FIFA WORLD CLUB CHAMPS. — GROUP B

TEAM	P	W	D	L	GF	GA	PTS
VASCO DA GAMA	3	3	0	0	8	3	9
NECAXA	3	1	1	1	5	4	4
MANCHESTER UNITED	3	1	1	1	4	4	4
SOUTH MELBOURNE	3	0	0	3	1	7	0

P=played; W=won; D=drawn; L=lost; GF=goals for; GA=goals against; PTS=points

1999-2000 RESULTS

FLIXPIX

DATE	OPPOSITION	COMPETITION	VENUE	RESULT	UNITED SCORERS
01/08/99	Arsenal	Charity Shield	Wembley	1-2	Beckham
08/08/99	Everton	Premier League	Goodison Park	1-1	Yorke
11/08/99	Sheffield Wednesday	Premier League	Old Trafford	4-0	Scholes, Yorke, Cole, Solskjaer
14/08/99	Leeds United	Premier League	Old Trafford	2-0	Yorke (2)
22/08/99	Arsenal	Premier League	Old Trafford	2-1	Keane (2)
25/08/99	Coventry City	Premier League	Highfield Road	2-1	Scholes, Yorke
27/08/99	Lazio	European Super Cup	Monaco	0-1	–
30/08/99	Newcastle United	Premier League	Old Trafford	5-1	Cole (4), Giggs
11/09/99	Liverpool	Premier League	Anfield	3-2	Own Goals (2), Cole
14/09/99	Croatia Zagreb	Champion's League	Old Trafford	0-0	–
18/09/99	Wimbledon	Premier League	Old Trafford	1-1	Cruyff
22/09/99	Sturm Graz	Champion's League	Graz, Austria	3-0	Keane, Cole, Yorke
25/09/99	Southampton	Premier League	Old Trafford	3-3	Sheringham, Yorke (2)
29/09/99	Marseilles	Champion's League	Old Trafford	2-1	Cole, Scholes
03/10/99	Chelsea	Premier League	Stamford Bridge	0-5	–
13/10/99	Aston Villa	Worthington Cup	Villa Park	0-3	–
16/10/99	Watford	Premier League	Old Trafford	4-1	Yorke, Cole (2), Irwin
19/10/99	Marseilles	Champion's League	Marseille, France	0-1	–
23/10/99	Tottenham Hotspur	Premier League	White Hart Lane	1-3	Giggs
27/10/99	Croatia Zagreb	Champion's League	Zagreb, Croatia	2-1	Beckham, Keane
30/10/99	Aston Villa	Premier League	Old Trafford	3-0	Scholes, Cole, Keane
02/11/99	Strum Graz	Champion's League	Old Trafford	2-1	Solskjaer, Keane
06/11/99	Leicester City	Premier League	Old Trafford	2-0	Cole (2)
20/11/99	Derby County	Premier League	Pride Park	2-1	Butt, Cole
23/11/99	Fiorentina	Champion's League	Florence, Italy	0-2	–
30/11/99	Palmeiras	World Club Cup	Tokyo, Japan	1-0	Keane
04/12/99	Everton	Premier League	Old Trafford	5-1	Irwin (pen), Solskjaer (4)
08/12/99	Valencia	Champion's League	Old Trafford	3-0	Keane, Solskjaer, Scholes
18/12/99	West Ham	Premier League	Boleyn Ground	4-2	Yorke (2), Giggs (2)
26/12/99	Bradford City	Premier League	Old Trafford	4-0	Fortune, Yorke, Cole, Keane
28/12/99	Sunderland	Premier League	Stadium of Light	2-2	Keane, Butt
06/01/00	Necaxa	World Club Champs.	Brazil	1-1	Yorke
08/01/00	Vasco da Gama	World Club Champs.	Brazil	1-3	Butt
11/01/00	South Melbourne	World Club Champs.	Brazil	2-0	Fortune (2)
24/01/00	Arsenal	Premier League	Old Trafford	1-1	Sheringham
29/01/00	Middlesbrough	Premier League	Old Trafford	1-0	Beckham
02/02/00	Sheffield Wednesday	Premier League	Hillsborough	1-0	Sheringham
05/02/00	Coventry City	Premier League	Old Trafford	3-2	Cole (2), Scholes
12/02/00	Newcastle United	Premier League	St James' Park	0-3	–
20/02/00	Leeds United	Premier League	Elland Road	1-0	Cole
26/02/00	Wimbledon	Premier League	Selhurst Park	2-2	Cruyff, Cole
01/03/00	Bordeaux	Champion's League	Old Trafford	2-0	Giggs, Sheringham
04/03/00	Liverpool	Premier League	Old Trafford	1-1	Solskjaer
07/03/00	Bordeaux	Champion's League	Bordeaux, France	2-1	Keane, Solskjaer
11/03/00	Derby County	Premier League	Old Trafford	3-1	Yorke (3)
15/03/00	Fiorentina	Champion's League	Old Trafford	3-1	Cole, Keane, Yorke
18/03/00	Leicester City	Premier League	Filbert Street	2-0	Beckham, Yorke
21/03/00	Valencia	Champion's League	Valencia, Spain	0-0	–
25/03/00	Bradford City	Premier League	Valley Parade	4-0	Yorke (2), Scholes, Beckham
01/04/00	West Ham	Premier League	Old Trafford	7-1	Scholes (3), Irwin, Cole, Beckham, Solskjaer
04/04/00	Real Madrid	Champion's League	Madrid, Spain	0-0	–
08/04/00	Middlesbrough	Premier League	Riverside Stadium	4-3	Giggs, Cole, Scholes, Fortune
15/04/00	Sunderland	Premier League	Old Trafford	4-0	Solskjaer (2), Butt, Berg
19/04/00	Real Madrid	Champion's League	Old Trafford	2-3	Beckham, Scholes (pen)
22/04/00	Southampton	Premier League	The Dell	3-1	Beckham, Solskjaer, Own Goal
24/04/00	Chelsea	Premier League	Old Trafford	3-2	Yorke (2), Solskjaer
29/04/00	Watford	Premier League	Vicarage Road	3-2	Yorke, Giggs, Cruyff
06/05/00	Tottenham Hotspur	Premier League	Old Trafford	3-1	Solskjaer, Beckham, Sheringham
14/05/00	Aston Villa	Premier League	Villa Park	1-0	Sheringham

BELOW (from top): Becks after his superb solo effort in the 3-2 defeat by Real Madrid; Teddy Sheringham on his way to scoring against Tottenham at Old Trafford; Ryan Giggs shoots on the Villa goal in the season's last game.

So you think you

This Manchester United quiz is split into three sections. Part One is relatively easy and most of the answers can be found somewhere in this annual, while Part Two is a little more difficult. Part Three will test your knowledge of Manchester United and their opponents to the limit, so let's see just how much you know about United!

PART 1 - NICE 'N' EASY!

1. What is the name of David Beckham's baby boy?
2. Which Manchester United player captained England schoolboys at cricket when he was younger?
3. Who did United beat 2-1 in the Champion's League Final to complete the famous Treble in 1999?
4. In which city was Andy Cole born?
5. With which team did Sir Alex Ferguson win the Scottish Championship?
6. What is Manchester United's nickname?
7. Who scored 'the greatest ever goal' in 1999's FA Cup Semi-Final replay and who were the opposition?
8. Which United player hails from the land down under?
9. Dwight Yorke was born on 3 November 1971. What star sign is he?
10. Paul Scholes scored England's second goal in the 1998 World Cup. Who were the opposition?

PART 2 - CHALLENGING!

1. Who holds United's all time goalscoring record with 199 goals?
2. Who was the keeper who was beaten by David Beckham from the halfway line at Selhurst Park in 1996?
3. Where was the 1999/2000 Champion's League Final held?
4. Which United player was sent off in the FIFA World Club Championships in Brazil and who were the opposition?
5. Which team became the first to beat Manchester United in a competitive match in 1999? What was the occasion, when and where did it take place and what was the score?
6. Which United player appeared in the Semi Finals of the 1998 World Cup?
7. What is Becks' wife famous for?
8. How many goals did the Andy Cole/ Dwight Yorke striking partnership score between them in the whole of the 1999/2000 season?
9. What hair care product is endorsed by David Beckham?
10. What nationality is Quinton Fortune?

know United?

PART 3 - THE REAL TEST!

1. Against which Premier League team did Ole Gunnar Solskjaer score 4 goals in 15 minutes after coming on as a substitute in February 1999?
2. Who managed United to their first European Cup triumph in 1968?
3. On which Formula One racing car might you have seen WWW.MANUTD.COM this year?
4. Which ex-United player is now thrilling the crowd at Ibrox for Scottish giants Rangers?
5. Gary and Phil Neville's sister Tracey is an England international in which sport?
6. In 1994 a Manchester United player became the first foreign recipient of the PFA Player of the Year award. Who was he?
7. There are six players who have scored 100 or more Premier League goals. Andy Cole is one of them, can you name the other five?
8. What was Manchester United's lowest League finish in the 1990s?
9. Who scored United's goals in the 3-1 victory over Fiorentina at Old Trafford in the Champion's League on 15th March 2000?
10. How many managers have been in the Old Trafford hot seat since 1945? Try to name some or all of them. If you know every one you can claim to be United's No. 1 Fan!

EXTRA TIME! - PLAYING AWAY

United don't just play their league games at Old Trafford, they also have to travel to the home grounds of the 19 other Premier League teams below. Can you name their grounds?

ARSENAL, ASTON VILLA, BRADFORD CITY, CHARLTON ATHLETIC, CHELSEA, COVENTRY CITY, DERBY COUNTY, EVERTON, IPSWICH TOWN, LEEDS UNITED, LEICESTER CITY, LIVERPOOL, MANCHESTER CITY, MIDDLESBROUGH, NEWCASTLE UNITED, SOUTHAMPTON, SUNDERLAND, TOTTENHAM HOTSPUR, WEST HAM UNITED

CHAMPIONS

... AGAIN & AGAIN

FAST FACT When Andy Cole scored three times against Feyenoord in the UEFA Champion's League in 1997 he became the first United player to notch a hat-trick in Europe for 30 years!

& AGAIN & AGAIN & AGAIN

CARLING CHAMPIONS
... AGAIN & AGAIN & AGAIN & AGAIN & AGAIN ...

CARLING CHAMPIONS

***ON THESE PAGES:* United celebrate winning the 1999/2000 Premier League title after the 3-1 victory over Spurs**

Colour in Ryan!

Colour in this picture of Ryan Giggs using paints, crayons or coloured pencils.

If you like you can send your completed picture to Fred the Red at Manchester United Football Club, Old Trafford, Manchester M16 0RA. Give it your best shot and Good Luck!

SHAPE UP!

Below are four pictures of some of your United favourites, but something seems to have gone wrong in the photographer's darkroom and now all that we can see of the players is their silhouettes. See if you can work out which player is which and check your answers on Page 64 to see if you are right!

Join the Club!

Do you want to become part of the biggest and best football club in the world? Of course you do and here's how!

JUNIOR MEMBERS

If you are one of Fred the Red's biggest fans and would love to join him in his fanatical support of the Old Trafford Reds, become a **JUNIOR MEMBER** for just £10 a year (UK only). When you join you will be sent three mailings throughout the football season and qualify for all the fantastic benefits below! In the first mailing, you will receive:

- Your Own Personalised Membership Card
- 2000/2001 Season Contract
  Signed by Sir Alex Ferguson and Fred the Red
- Exclusive United Poster and Results Wallchart
- Free Copy of the Manchester United Yearbook

As a **JUNIOR MEMBER** you will not only belong to the biggest and best football club in the world, you will also be able to take advantage of these amazing offers:

- Priority in Ordering Match Tickets
  Being a **Junior Member** does not guarantee a Match Day ticket, but it does give you priority in ordering tickets for United's home games. Details can be found in the Match Ticket Application Book which will arrive with your first mailing. NB: Remember, anyone wanting to come to a game with you must also be a Manchester United Member.
- Free Admission to ALL Reserve Team Home Games
- Half-Price Museum and Stadium Tours
- 10% Discount on Official Merchandise
  At the Manchester United Megastore and via Manchester United Direct
- 10% Discount on Match Programme Subscription
- 10% Discount at the Red Café
- Away Travel Club Membership
  Junior Members are enrolled in the Manchester United Away Travel Club, which means that you can book travel organised by the Membership Office to away games in the UK and Europe.
- Personal Life Insurance
  Junior Members are covered by life insurance while travelling to or attending United League and Cup matches in the UK and Ireland. Details can be found in the Members Benefits Booklet which will arrive with your first mailing.

To find out more on becoming a Junior Member call 0161 868 8450 or write to: Manchester United Membership Office, Manchester United Football Club, Old Trafford, Manchester M16 0RA. Go on ... start pestering your mum and dad for a stamp!

THE BOSS!

It is hard to believe that after four years in charge at Old Trafford, Sir Alex Ferguson's future was very much in doubt and many fans wanted him to go ... oh, how times have changed!

Born in the Govan area of Glasgow, Scotland, on the last day of 1941, the young Alex Ferguson was a football-mad supporter of Glasgow Rangers. He was rought up among the fiercely passionate shipbuilding ommunity which flourished on the River Clyde both during nd after the Second World War. At 16, while serving an pprenticeship as a toolmaker, he joined amateur Scottish ide Queen's Park, who played their home matches at the ıtimidating Hampden Park. Alex went on to play up front for t Johnstone, Dunfermline and, for two and a half years 1967-69), for the team he supported as a boy, Rangers, nding his first season there as top goalscorer with 23 goals. lso in 1967, he represented Scotland on their summer tour, coring 10 goals in games against Israel, Hong Kong Select, ustralia (3 games), Auckland Provincial XI and the Vancouver All Stars. Alex's time at Rangers was ultimately unfulfilling and in 1969 he left to join Second Division Falkirk. After four years at Brockville and a final year of playing at Ayr United, Fergie began his managerial career in July 1974 at Second Division East Stirlingshire.

In just three months, Alex transformed the team, raising it from the bottom of the Second Division up to fourth place, then moving on to fresh challenges with St Mirren in Paisley. He lead the Saints to the Division One Title in 1977 and consolidated their position in the Premier Division the following year. After his dismissal, he joined Aberdeen in May 1978. It was here at Pittodrie, that Alex Ferguson's managerial reputation was firmly established, when he broke the dominance of the Glasgow giants, Celtic and

Continued on Page 48 ➛

Rangers. In the club's entire history up to 1978, Aberdeen had collected only 7 trophies, just one of which was a League Championship in 1954-55. During the eight years Alex managed the team, Aberdeen won a total of 12 titles, including 3 League Championships, 4 Scottish Cups and a fantastic European Cup Winner's Cup title in 1983. Ferguson had proved himself a truly great manager, able to transform a team's fortunes both on and off the pitch. There followed a brief spell as caretaker manager of the Scottish national team at the World Cup Finals in Mexico in 1986, when he took over from his great friend and hero Jock Stein who tragically collapsed and died during a qualifier against Wales.

At this time, Manchester United were a struggling and dispirited side under manager Ron Atkinson. In November 1986, three months into the season, they were languishing near the foot of the First Division table. After approaches from Rangers, Barcelona, Arsenal and Spurs, Alex Ferguson became the manager of Manchester United on 6 November 1986. He knew that to be a success at Old Trafford he would have to end the 19 year wait for the League Championship title. His first game in charge clearly showed the massive challenge ahead as his team lost 2-0 against Oxford United.

He began, as he had at Aberdeen and St Mirren, by re-inventing the club as a whole, right down to the very last detail. He placed extra demands on his players, controlling their diet and enforcing a strict training regime. He also established an efficient youth system. Sir Alex was worried that complacency had set in, as there were no young, gifted players coming through to challenge the established First Teamers. This was a long-term task and in the meantime, United needed to be saved from the very real threat of relegation. Without adding to the squad, he guided them to 11th place that first season. The next year he delved into the transfer market and with his new signings, like stalwarts Brian McClair and Steve Bruce, United finished a remarkable second. However, there was still much to do and 11th and 13th place finishes in 1988/89 and 1989/90 respectively, followed by a disappointing start to the next league campaign, heaped pressure on the United board to make a change. This was Alex's "Black December" and it has been said that without Manchester United's FA Cup run that season and the eventual 1-0 triumph over Crystal Palace in the Final replay, he may not have survived as manager. Most of the credit for the club's patience with Alex must go to Sir Bobby Charlton, who championed Fergie's appointment and stayed faithful to his manager through those difficult days. With the FA Cup in the bag, United pushed forward, hungry for success. Mark Hughes' wondergoal against Barcelona clinched the European Cup Winner's Cup trophy in 1991 and a 1-0 victory over Nottingham Forest in the League Cup Final the next season earned United their third domestic trophy in three years. By now the fans were desperate for the League title, not won since 1967. Leeds just beat them to the Championship in 1992, thanks in part, to an enigmatic Frenchman called Eric Cantona and a last day own goal by Sheffield United's Brian Gayle.

The next year, the first of the breakaway Premier League United were not to be denied. Alex pulled off an amazing coup by tempting Cantona from Leeds to Old Trafford and with 'King Eric' at the heart of the team, United proved unstoppable. They carried the championship-winning form of 1992/93 into the next season and, aided by new signing Roy Keane, looked on course for a unique domestic treble. However, some new year 'wobbles' resulted in League Cup final defeat by Aston Villa and their 16-point lead in the title race almost disappeared. However, Alex and United regained their composure and finished the 1993/94 season as only the fourth team in the modern era, (after Spurs, Arsenal and Liverpool) to claim a League Championship and FA Cup double. Alex also retained the Manager of the Year award he won the previous season. 1994/95 ended trophyless despite the £7 million signing of Andy Cole, as his first United

'Until my dying day, I shall be grateful to Manchester United for all my association with the club has given me. For someone who loves football as much as I do, there is no better place to be.'
***SIR ALEX FERGUSON* (taken from his autobiography, *Managing My Life*)**

team fell one point short in the title race and one goal short in the FA Cup Final with Everton. There was also the infamous Eric Cantona "kung fu kick" episode at Selhurst Park which saw United on the front and back pages of most newspapers for weeks, and saw the Frenchman banned for 9 months.

In the summer before the 1995/96 season, Alex sold crowd favourites Mark Hughes, Paul Ince and Andrei Kanchelskis and replaced them with the first crop of youngsters from the new youth system he had established in his early days at Old Trafford. David Beckham, Paul Scholes, Ryan Giggs, Nicky Butt and Gary and Phil Neville may well be household names now, but after losing the first game of that season, most observers agreed with Alan Hansen's comment: 'You win nothing with kids!' However, this season propelled Alex Ferguson into the "Great Manager" bracket. His United team, half of them under 21 and former Youth Team players, grabbed a second double triumph, and the returning Eric Cantona scored the only goal in the FA Cup Final victory over Liverpool.

Ole Gunnar Solskjaer and Ronny Johnsen came to Old Trafford for the 1996/97 season and almost inevitably, United won their fourth Premier League Championship in five years. Fergie's next challenge was the European Cup, last won by the legendary Matt Busby in 1968. United's semi-final defeat in 1997 by Borussia Dortmund (the eventual winners) was hard to bear, especially as United had looked the better side; but it was the closest United had come for nearly thirty years. Alex added Teddy Sheringham to his squad for the 1997/98 season and although United finished the year empty-handed, with Arsenal completing their own "double double", the Old Trafford squad was looking strong.

Fergie added Dwight Yorke and Jaap Stam to his team at the start of 1998/99 and, with Roy Keane back from long-term injury and David Beckham producing the best football of his career, United pressed forward on three fronts – Premier League, FA Cup and Champion's League. Achieving this truly remarkable treble is without doubt the finest managerial triumph of all time. There were many occasions throughout the season when teams with a lesser guiding force than that of Sir Alex Ferguson would have folded, not least when 2-0 down to Juventus at the Stadio delle Alpi in the Champion's League semi-final. There are many examples of Sir Alex Ferguson's fantastic leadership – such as his superb handling of Becks after he was sent off in France 98; his clever use of the entire United squad during a punishing 61-game season, which enabled the team to function at 100% throughout; and the devastating effect of his substitutions in the FA Cup and Champion's League Finals.

One of the major aspects of Fergie's career is his obvious desire for success. With the Treble completed and his fledgling team established as international superstars, he could have been forgiven for resting on his laurels. This was not to be! With Mark Bosnich taking over from the irreplaceable Peter Schmeichel in goal, United began the 1999/2000 season committed to retaining the Premier League and Champion's League crowns.

United's defence of the FA Cup was denied by the withdrawa[l] which allowed them to take part in the inaugural and, in the event, ill-fated FIFA World Club Championships in Brazil. Despite the pressure created by Leeds and Arsenal, United collected their sixth Premier League title in eight years. Fergie's team, however, could not repeat the Champion's League success of the previous year, going out to eventual winners Real Madrid in the Quarter Finals.

Sir Alex Ferguson has proved himself again and again in the 14 years he has managed Manchester United. He has built at least two distinct teams and laid the foundations for many years of future success at Old Trafford. He has won the Manager of the Year award no less than six times and in a poll of Premiership Managers in March 2000 he was voted the greatest manager of all time. In the 2000 New Year's Honours List he became the first working football manager to be knighted and he is also the only man to have managed championship-winning teams in both England and Scotland.

During his time in Manchester, United has become the biggest sporting outfit in the world with a turnover of over £1 billion and Old Trafford has grown to an 80,000 capacity, the largest club ground in Britain. The list of his achievements is immense and yet the desire to continue succeeding burns as brightly as ever. To those who shouted for his dismissal in December 1990 the question is: Where are you now?

FERGIE'S TROPHIES AS A MANAGER

AT ST MIRREN (1974-1978)		
Scottish Division One Titles	1	(1977)
AT ABERDEEN (1978 – 1986)		
Scottish League Titles	3	(1980, 1984, 1985)
European Cup Winner's Cup	1	(1983)
Scottish FA Cup	4	(1982, 1983, 1984, 1986)
Scottish League Cup	2	(1986)
Scottish Drybrough Cup	1	(1981)
European Super Cup	1	(1983)
AT MANCHESTER UNITED (1986 –		
Champion's League	1	(1999)
Premier League Titles	6	(1993, 1994, 1996, 1997, 1999, 2000)
FA Cup	4	(1990, 1994, 1996, 1999)
World Club/Intercontinental Cup	1	(1999)
European Cup Winner's Cup	1	(1991)
European Super Cup	1	(1991)
League Cup	1	(1992)
Charity Shield	5	(1990 (joint), 1993, 1994, 1996, 1997)
GRAND TOTAL	**33**	

GOAL KING COLE!

When Sir Alex Ferguson broke the transfer record by paying £7 million to Kevin Keegan at Newcastle for Andy Cole, most United fans thought they were getting a natural goalscorer, but Coley is much, much more than that!

One of only six players to have bagged 100 or more goals in the Premier League, he has been a consistent goalscorer throughout his career and has maintained an average of one goal every two games, the benchmark of a truly great striker. The sheer number of chances that Coley gets is due more to his electrifying pace and instinct for a goalscoring chance than anything else. His partnership with Dwight Yorke over the past two seasons has reaped huge rewards for Manchester United, some of their combination play has been absolutely awesome, particularly in the Nou Camp against Barcelona in the Champion's League on 25 November 1998. In the Champion's League encounter with Fiorentina at Old Trafford on 15 March 2000, United needed a win to ensure progression to the knock-out stages. Andy not only scored a sublime equaliser, he also cleverly pulled out wide on the left throughout the game, allowing Ryan Giggs to terrify the Italian defence through the middle. This helped stretch the Fiorentina back line to such an extent that Roy Keane and Dwight Yorke sealed a 3-1 victory.

Andy Cole began his career at the National School of Excellence at Lilleshall (now superceded by the FA Premier League Football Academies) and then signed schoolboy forms at Arsenal. After loan spells at Fulham and Bristol City, he joined First Division Bristol City for £500,000 in July 1992. Eight months and 12 goals later, Cole was snapped up by Kevin Keegan, then Newcastle United manager, for £1,750,000. He became an instant success on Tyneside,

bagging 12 league goals before the end of the 1992/93 season and helping Newcastle gain promotion to the Premier League. His first season in the top flight was nothing short of phenomenal. Scoring 34 league goals earnt him the European Golden Boot and he was awarded the PFA Young Player of the Year award.

The following season Andy continued his good goalscoring form and had already scored 9 in the Premier League when Sir Alex Ferguson's offer of £6,250,000 together with Keith Gillespie persuaded Kevin Keegan to part company with the man they call "Goal King Cole". Andy arrived at Old Trafford on 12 January 1995 as United were gunning for their third consecutive title. He began well and on 4 March he grabbed an amazing five goals in the 9-0 demolition of Ipswich. However, the season ended badly for Coley as United failed to beat West Ham on the last day of the season, handing Blackburn, who lost at Anfield, the Premier League title. Andy Cole was blamed for this failure as he missed many gilt-edged opportunities at Upton Park, any one of which would have won the game and taken United above Blackburn.

Andy showed his true quality and commendable temperament during the following campaign as he helped guide the young United side to the Premier League and FA Cup double. His goalscoring tally was slightly lower than his previous two seasons but his all round play was significantly improved as the excellent coaching skills of Sir Alex

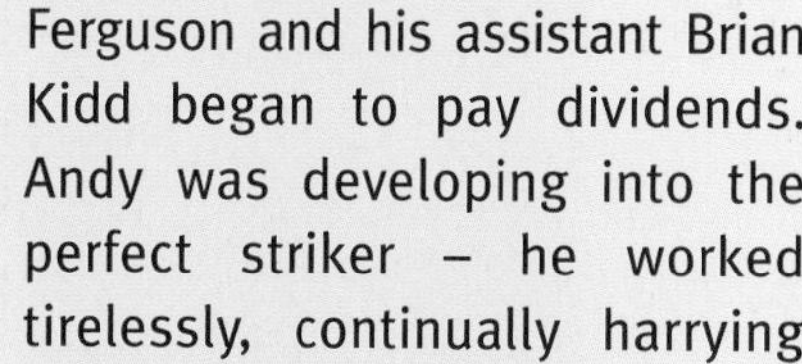

Ferguson and his assistant Brian Kidd began to pay dividends. Andy was developing into the perfect striker – he worked tirelessly, continually harrying opposition defenders and his pacy runs opened up gaps in the opponent's rearguard which the likes of Paul Scholes and Roy Keane were able to exploit. He also made amends for the West Ham game by scoring in the 3-0 defeat of Middlesbrough which confirmed United as Premier League champions. Illness and two broken legs at the start of the 1996/97 season kept him out of the team until December and with new signing Ole Gunnar Solskjaer in unstoppable form, his First Team outings were limited and he spent a lot of time on the substitutes bench. Two goals in a week in April 1997 and a superb hat-trick in the 7-0 drubbing of Barnsley in October proved that Andy was back to full form and fitness. However, another hat-trick in the Champion's League against Feyenoord later in the season and other electrifying displays were not enough to earn him a place in the England squad for the 1998 World Cup.

When Dwight Yorke joined United for the start of the Treble season, many thought Andy Cole may have to step aside. As it turned out, this could not have been further from the truth as the two players established an almost telepathic partnership which bamboozled defences throughout Europe. The deadly duo ended that momentous season with an incredible 53 goals between them. Andy had also scored the winning goal against Spurs in the last Premiership game of the season with a deft chip over Ian Walker to take the title to Old Trafford.

The Cole and Yorke combination was firing on all cylinders at the beginning of the 1999/2000 campaign. Both scored in the first league game at Old Trafford in a 4-0 victory over Sheffield Wednesday and although Cole didn't score for another 4 games, when he did, it was well worth waiting for. His old side Newcastle United visited Old Trafford with Ruud Gullit in charge and the Magpies left with their tails well and truly between their legs as Cole bagged four goals and set up Ryan Giggs for the fifth in a 5-1 victory. He continued scoring regularly throughout the season, including braces at Old Trafford against Watford, Leicester and Coventry. He also scored the crucial winner in the top-of-the-table crunch game against Leeds at Elland Road in February, taking the ball smartly past Lucas Radebe and steering the ball beyond Nigel Martyn. Cole ended the year with an impressive 22 goals, taking his United total to 104 goals in just 197 games. ●

ANDY COLE

Full Name: Andrew Alexander Cole
Position: Forward
Date of Birth: 25 October 1971
Place of Birth: Nottingham
Height: 5'10"
Weight: 12st. 4lb.
Previous Clubs: Arsenal, Fulham (on loan) Bristol City, Newcastle United
United Debut: vs Arsenal at Wembley 9/8/98 (Charity Shield)
1st United Goal: vs Aston Villa at Old Trafford 4/2/95 (Premier League)
Total United Appearances: 197 (+32 as sub)
Total United Goals: 104

BETWEEN THE

One of the biggest talking points at the start of the 1999/2000 season was how United were going to replace the awesome presence of Peter Schmeichel in goal.

August 1999 saw Manchester United start a new season for the first time in 9 years without the "Great Dane", Peter Schmeichel, between the sticks. Sir Alex Ferguson looked to replace him by signing two goalkeepers to join Raimond Van Der Gouw, who had served as cover for Schmeichel since he joined from Vitesse Arnhem in June 1996. Mark Bosnich came to Old Trafford under the Bosman ruling, with no transfer fee involved, after an acrimonious last few months at Aston Villa. The Villa fans accused him of being mercenary, deliberately not signing a contract at Villa Park in order to secure a lucrative signing-on fee when he went to United in the summer. Massimo Taibi, on the other hand, quietly joined United early on in the season for £4.4 million from Italian Serie A side Venezia.

Mark Bosnich had started his football career at Old Trafford. As a youngster, he spent three years in United's Youth Team but work permit problems forced him to return to Australia. Shortly afterwards, Ron Atkinson, now manager of Aston Villa, solved those problems and brought him to Villa Park. By 1997, Mark was recognised as one of the best goalies in the Premier League, and he had a growing reputation as a penalty saver. With his contract nearing its expiry date in 1999, United headed a list of clubs desperate for his signature. So when Bosnich eventually joined United, he was seen as an able successor to Peter Schmeichel and hence he took the field in the season's curtain-raiser, the Charity Shield at Wembley against Arsenal. Strong performances followed, but in the Premier League game against Leeds, Mark aggravated an existing hamstring problem, forcing him out of the side. In fact, much of the early criticism levelled at Mark concerned his poor kicking and it was only later in the season that is was revealed that he had been "hamstrung" by the persistent injury that had flared up again in the Leeds game.

Sir Alex moved quickly when it became clear Bosnich may be out for some time. He swiftly brought the Italian goalie, Massimo Taibi to Old Trafford. Taibi settled in well and produced some fine performances in the League, while Raimond van der Gouw excelled in Europe – Taibi had signed too late and therefore was ineligible for the Champion's League. Even when Mark Bosnich was fit, he remained on the bench for some time while his goalkeeping colleagues made the most of their First Team chances. However, it was not long before Mark Bosnich became first choice once more, partly because of blunders by Taibi and Van der Gouw. Collecting a weak shot from Matt Le Tissier in the Premiership clash with Southampton on 25 September 1999, Taibi's studs somehow became wedged in the turf and the ball dribbled through his legs and into the net! This terrible mistake cost United 2 points in a 3-3 draw. Bosnich was back in the frame and produced a commanding display in the World Club Cup game against Palmeiras. So impressive was Bosnich, that Taibi was loaned to Italian club Cosenza, in order to get First Team action.

Van der Gouw still played in most Champion's League games even though Bosnich's form, which included a penalty save, was one of the few pluses from the disappointing FIFA World Championships in Brazil. However,

Raimond Van der Gouw

Mark Bosnich

Massimo Taibi

STICKS

in the Champion's League game with Bordeaux (on 7 March 2000), Rai dropped a fairly weak shot from Michel Pavon into the back of his own net and consequently, although United won the game 2-1, Mark Bosnich took over in goal in Europe as well. His performances in the Premier League were going from strength to strength and on the European stage, as the opposition became tougher, his displays became more commanding. In the first leg of the Champion's League Quarter-Final with Real Madrid at the Bernabeau Stadium, he was United's "man-of-the-match", producing a point-blank save from Steve McManaman to keep the score-sheet blank. Mark Bosnich's first season at Old Trafford may have been a difficult one, but he has shown a toughness and determination in re-claiming the Number 1 jersey that should ensure that Fabien Barthez will have to fight the Australian for the First Team place! In fact, Bosnich made it quite clear that, although Barthez had signed for a world record fee, his future was still at Old Trafford. ●

RAIMOND VAN DER GOUW
Born: 24 March 1963, Oldenzaal, Holland
Height: 6'3"
Weight: 13st. 3lb.
Previous Clubs: Go Ahead Eagles, Vitesse Arnhem
United Debut: vs Aston Villa 21/9/96
United Appearances: 38 (+4 as sub)

MARK BOSNICH
Born: 13 January 1972, Sydney, Australia
Height: 6'2"
Weight: 13st. 7lb.
Previous Clubs: Sydney Croatia, Aston Villa
United Debut: vs Arsenal 1/8/99
United Appearances: 35

MASSIMO TAIBI
Born: 18 February 1970, Palermo, Italy
Height: 6'1"
Weight: 13st. 5lb.
Previous Clubs: Licata, Trento, AC Milan, Como, Piacenza, Venezia
United Debut: vs Liverpool 11/9/99
United Appearances: 3

FRENCH CONNECTION

After much speculation in the newspapers, France's international keeper, Fabien Barthez, joined United on 1 June 2000 from Monaco for a world record fee for a goalkeeper of £7.8 million. One of the most colourful characters in world football, Barthez will be remembered as the goalkeeper who excelled in France's World Cup winning campaign on home soil in 1998, conceding only 2 goals in the tournament. One of the most memorable images from those championships was French captain Laurent Blanc kissing Fabien's bald head for luck prior to every game! And last summer we saw this same ritual as France collected the Euro 2000 trophy.

He began his career with Toulouse FC in 1989 before joining Olympic Marseille in 1992, helping the French south coast club to the European Cup in his first season. He made a move along the French Riviera to AS Monaco two years later. In 1997 he collected a League winner's medal with the club and the next year he was instrumental in Monaco's away goals victory over United in the Champion's League. Then came his World Cup triumph, followed in the 1999/2000 season with another league title with Monaco. Barthez is a winner, proved by his awesome domestic and international record. He also possesses an extremely extrovert personality and the comparisons with Peter Schmeichel are obvious. When he signed for United he summed up his appetite for the challenge at Old Trafford: 'My ambitions? To win, to win, to win. I want to stay here for a long time and I want to win. Simple as that!'

ROY KEANE

Full Name: Roy Maurice Keane
Position: Midfield
Date of Birth: 10 August 1971
Place of Birth: Cork, Republic of Ireland
Height: 5'10"
Weight: 12st. 2lb.
Previous Clubs: Cobh Ramblers, Nottingham Forest
United Debut: vs Norwich City at Carrow Road 15/8/95 (First Division)
1st United Goal: vs Aston Villa at Old Trafford 4/2/95 (Premier League)
Total United Appearances: 263 (+11 as sub)
Total United Goals: 39

Undoubtedly the biggest influence on the pitch, Manchester United club captain Roy Keane's appetite for success is equal to that of his manager.

KEANE AS

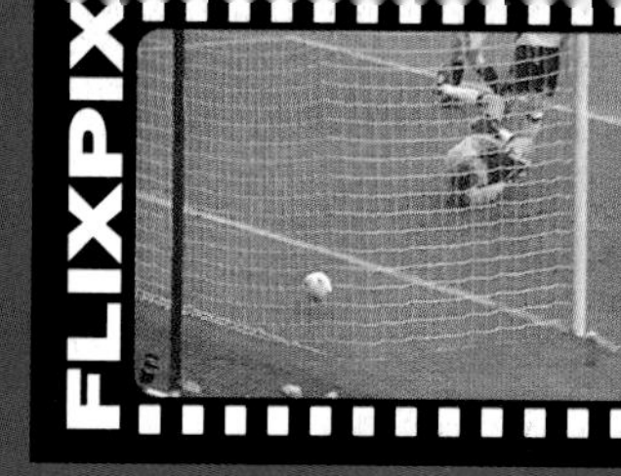

Roy Keane first came to the attention of Sir Alex Ferguson during his time at Nottingham Forest where he made his reputation as a highly skilled, tough-tackling midfield general who could also be relied upon to supply vital goals from the centre of the park. Signed from Cobh Rangers in Ireland for a mere £10,000 by the then Forest manager Brian Clough, he was soon a First Team regular at the City Ground and appeared in the FA Cup Final in 1991. Unfortunately, Roy was on the losing side as Spurs came from behind to win 2-1 and he was also unlucky the following year in the League Cup when his future employers Manchester United beat Forest in the final. Keano's star was rising just as Nottingham Forest's was falling and when the team was relegated in 1992/93 there was no way they were able to hold on to their star midfielder. There followed protracted wrangling over his signature as Nottingham Forest looked to cash in on the man who had become the hottest property in English football. United eventually beat Blackburn Rovers to the chase and signed Roy for a British record transfer fee of £3,750,000 in the summer of 1993.

At the time, the United midfield was being bossed by the man known as "the Guv'nor", Paul Ince, and for the next two years, Keane's First Team opportunities were limited. However, the young Irishman was learning his trade all the while and when Ince left United in 1995 he moved effortlessly into the centre of the midfield and played as if he'd been there all his life. Roy Keane is not the typical defensive midfielder. Although he can tackle, track back and break up opposition attacks better than anyone else in the Premier League, he can also pass accurately, begin attacks, retain possession and steam forward into the opposition's penalty box like the most accomplished attacking midfielder. And he can do this for the full 90 minutes for 50 games a season. He is undoubtedly the most complete midfield player in the country.

With his guiding influence, United completed the double-double in 1995/96 and retained the Premier League title in 1996/97. However, just like the old cliché, Roy's importance to the United team could only be accurately judged when he wasn't there. The 1998/99 season may well have ended very differently if Roy had not missed most of it through a cruciate ligament injury. With Arsenal pushing United hard for the championship in the closing months of the campaign, Roy Keane's drive and enthusiasm in the heart of midfield was sorely missed and so it was the North Londoners who went on to claim the double. Roy was back to full fitness at the start of the Treble season and his consistent displays throughout did much to keep United gunning for all three trophies. He performed superbly in the Champion's League games, especially those away from home when the pressure was really on – the presence of Roy Keane battling away tirelessly just in front of the back four prevented opposition teams from sustaining any realistic challenge on the United goal. He also scored vital goals, none more so than United's first in the Champion's League Semi-Final Second Leg in Turin against Juventus. At 2-0 down, 3-1 on aggregate, United looked destined to fall short in Europe again until Roy's headed intervention. However, the 1998/99 season did have its lows for Roy as well as the wonderful highs – he was sent off in the FA Cup Semi-Final replay with Arsenal; a booking in the match against Juventus meant that he was suspended from the Champion's League Final and he finished the year back on the treatment table with an ankle injury sustained in the FA Cup Final. Despite these setbacks, no one could deny that United's success was due in no small part to the awesome performances from Captain Keane throughout the year.

The 1999/2000 season began with mounting speculation in the press about the future of Roy Keane. There was talk that United had refused to accept his wage demands and that Keane was unwilling to sign his new contract. The importance of his presence in the team was stressed by his two goals against Arsenal at Highbury which earned all three points for United in late August. With the crowd chanting for Roy to stay at every available opportunity, he eventually signed up to a deal that would make him the highest paid player in England. Most football people regard Roy Keane as worth every penny and he proved his worth over the course of this season against Arsenal, Sturm Graz, Croatia Zagreb, Aston Villa, Palmeiras, Valencia, Bradford City, Sunderland, Bordeaux and Fiorentina.

By the end of the season, Roy had grabbed 12 goals (6 of these in the Champion's League), making this his best goalscoring season ever. He also seems to have curbed some of the overly aggressive play that has got him into trouble in previous seasons, and his red and yellow card count has reduced. However, as far as his whole-hearted aggressive approach to football goes, Roy Keane sums it up accordingly when he says: 'I'll never change my game. It isn't possible. If I did I would be half the player that I am.' ●

MUSTARD

STARS OF THE UNITED SQUAD

With the increasing demands placed on successful teams like Manchester United, it has become vitally important to supplement the club's star players with equally effective squad players. The United squad is one of the finest in the world and here are the best of the bunch!

TEDDY SHERINGHAM

Teddy joined Manchester United from Tottenham Hotspur in the summer of 1997 for £3.5 million. He immediately added a new dimension to the United attack with his subtle skills and intelligent passing. His First Team chances have been limited but he found glory in the 1998/99 Treble-winning season: first, by scoring the opening goal in the FA Cup Final barely a minute after coming on as a sub; and secondly, with the 90th minute equaliser and then the flick header which set up Solskjaer's winner in the Champion's League Final a few days later. He has been a consistent performer in his time with United, scoring many valuable goals, and signed an extension to his contract in May 2000. It now seems likely that he will see out the end of his career at Old Trafford.

Position: Forward
Date of Birth: 2 April 1966
Place of Birth: Highams Park, Essex
Height: 6'1"
Weight: 12st. 8lb.
United Appearances: 68 (+42 as sub)
United Goals: 25
ENGLAND INTERNATIONAL

DENIS IRWIN

Denis is one of the unsung heroes of the United squad who has been at Old Trafford since his £650,000 move from Oldham Athletic in 1990. He has therefore been at Manchester United during all of Sir Alex Ferguson's "glory years", playing mostly in a left-back position although, when he joined initially, slotted into a right-back role. His versatility and consistency in defence have kept this likeable Irishman at the heart of United's success. Irwin is also prepared to push forward to help the attack and he possesses a fearsome shot which, together with his penalty-taking duties, has allowed him to amass a goalscoring total that is enviable for a defender.

Position: Defender
Date of Birth: 31 October 1965
Place of Birth: Cork, Ireland
Height: 5'8"
Weight: 10st. 10lb.
United Appearances: 463 (+13 as sub)
United Goals: 31
REP. OF IRELAND INTERNATIONAL

OLE GUNNAR SOLSKJAER

The "baby-faced assassin" scored on his debut for United and hasn't looked back. Although his First Team chances have been limited, he has had some marvellous moments in the Red shirt, mostly when coming off the substitutes bench. He scored the winning strike in the 1999 Champion's League Final against Bayern Munich in Barcelona, and twice, he has scored four goals in the Premiership – he is the only player ever to do so. Ole further endeared himself to the United fans in the summer of 1999 when he turned down a £5.5 million transfer and the chance of regular First Team action at Spurs to remain at Old Trafford.

Position: Forward
Date of Birth: 26 February 1973
Place of Birth: Kristiansund, Norway
Height: 5'9"
Weight: 11st. 9lb.
United Appearances: 93 (+66 as sub)
United Goals: 61
NORWEGIAN INTERNATIONAL

RONNY JOHNSEN

Ronny has excelled for United since his arrival from Turkish side Besiktas on 29 July 1996. Already an established world class defender, he quickly adapted to English football. His assets include startling acceleration, pace and strength in the air. He also possesses immense skill as a man marker, both in defence and further up the park in midfield. Johnsen has performed superbly when asked to keep an eye on quality players like Zinedine Zidane in tough European encounters. A long term injury lay-off during the 1999/2000 season was unfortunate but, back to full fitness, he will prove, again, to be one of Alex Ferguson's shrewdest investments yet.

Position: Defender
Date of Birth: 10 June 1969
Place of Birth: Norway
Height: 6'2"
Weight: 13st. 2lb.
United Appearances: 97 (+17 as sub)
United Goals: 7
NORWEGIAN INTERNATIONAL

HENNING BERG

Sir Alex Ferguson had already tried and failed to bring Henning Berg to Old Trafford when the Norwegian joined Kenny Dalglish at Blackburn Rovers in 1991. Henning soon established himself as one of the best Premiership defenders and was an integral part of Rovers' Championship winning side of 1994/95. When he arrived at United in the summer of 1997 for £5 million, he quickly endeared himself to the fans with outstanding performances alongside Gary Pallister at centre back. However, the arrival of Jaap Stam at the start of the 1998/99 season and the form of Ronny Johnsen, meant Berg often found himself on the substitutes bench. He has played a vital role in United's success over the last few years though, especially in European competition, with Johnsen's long-term injury in 1999 allowing Berg to develop a great understanding with Jaap Stam at the heart of United's rearguard.

Position: Defender
Date of Birth: 1 September 1969
Place of Birth: Eidsvell, Norway
Height: 6'0"
Weight: 12st. 1lb.
United Appearances: 81 (+21 as sub)
United Goals: 3
NORWEGIAN INTERNATIONAL

QUINTON FORTUNE

This young South African came to the attention of Sir Alex Ferguson while playing for Atletico Madrid in Spain. He joined United for £1.5 million in the summer of 1999. He is a talented left sided attacking midfielder who, for most of his time at Old Trafford, has served as backup for Ryan Giggs. He scored both goals in the 2-0 victory over South Melbourne in the FIFA World Club Championship in January 2000 and certainly looks to have a great future at United.

Position: Midfield
Date of Birth: 21 May 1977
Place of Birth: Cape Town, S. Africa
Height: 5'11"
Weight: 11st. 11lb.
United Appearances: 6 (+6 as sub)
United Goals: 4
SOUTH AFRICAN INTERNATIONAL

WES BROWN

Manchester born Wes Brown is one of the latest crop of exciting young players to come off the Old Trafford production line. With such a wealth of existing defensive talent, Wes has not yet gained a regular First Team place, but his outstanding qualities mark him out as a great prospect for the future. In fact, he has already received international recognition by claiming his first England cap in the Friendly with Hungary in Budapest on 28 April 1998 after only 12 appearances in the United First Team! Wes has also demonstrated his versatility by deputising, not only in his preferred centre back role, but as a makeshift full back. With his strength and pace Wes Brown is sure to have a very bright future at Old Trafford.

Position: Defender
Date of Birth: 13 October 1979
Place of Birth: Manchester
Height: 6'1"
Weight: 11st. 11lb.
United Appearances: 17 (+6 as sub)
United Goals: 2
ENGLAND INTERNATIONAL

NICKY BUTT

Nicky Butt is another of the talented young players to have graduated through Manchester United's Youth Team ranks, making his First Team debut as long ago as 1992. However, it wasn't until 1994 that he staked his claim for a regular senior place. This ferocious midfielder who bites into tackles and disrupts opposition attacks is also adept at linking defence and attack with pinpoint passes and clever running. He scores his fair share of goals, but his most outstanding quality is his limitless energy, which allows him to maintain a very high level of performance for 90 minutes, week in, week out. His opportunities in the First Team have been limited over the past three years due mostly to the excellent form of Roy Keane and Paul Scholes. However, when called upon, like he was during Roy Keane's absence through injury for the closing stages of the 1997/98 season and in the 1999 Champion's League Final, he rarely disappoints.

Position: Midfield
Date of Birth: 21 January 1975
Place of Birth: Manchester
Height: 5'10"
Weight: 11st. 5lb.
United Appearances: 198 (+48 as sub)
United Goals: 19
ENGLAND INTERNATIONAL

SHOP TILL YOU DROP!

One of the biggest success stories of recent years has been the explosion in Manchester United merchandising which has brought all the fun and excitement of supporting United to fans all over the globe. It has also boosted the value of Manchester United as a whole, so that the club is now worth in excess of £1 billion – officially the world's biggest football club!

At Old Trafford itself is the awesome new **Manchester United Megastore**, opened in July 2000, which has a sales area of some 18,000 square feet. Here there is a full range of fantastic Manchester United goodies. These include all the club kit, child and adult clothing, videos, music, books, toys, clocks, watches, wallpaper, duvet covers, footballs and a whole lot more – you name it, the Megastore has it! And remember, the Manchester United Megastore is committed to quality, so you can be sure that anything you buy will be of the highest possible standard and you are protected by a no-nonsense, money-back guarantee if you are not satisfied. While you shop, you can also catch up with some of the latest action from your United stars as the club's official digital channel, MUTV, is shown on screens throughout the store.

If you're planning a day out at Old Trafford on a non-match day to tour the stadium [see Pages 6 & 7] and plan to visit the Megastore, then you could time your trip to coincide with one of the special events which are regularly organised there. Keep a look out in official United publications, like the matchday programme, Glory Glory, the Fred the Red comic and the official Manchester United magazine, and check out the club's website for details of when some of your favourite stars, celebrities and even Fred the Red will be there.

You can also visit the Manchester United Megastore on-line from the comfort of your own home – via the official website –**WWW.MANUTD.COM**. Here you can check out all the latest official club goodies and have them delivered direct to your door. Isn't technology amazing!

Manchester United has millions of supporters throughout the world and not all of them can visit Old Trafford or have access to the internet to shop on-line. For these fans, United has embarked on an ambitious expansion plan, bringing the taste of Old Trafford to all supporters wherever they are. On 29 October 1998 the first official Manchester United store outside of Old Trafford was launched at Dublin Airport in Eire. Such was its success, that in August 1999 a similar store was opened at Gatwick Airport in the south-east of England. Manchester United stores have since opened in Abu Dhabi in the United Arab Emirates and Singapore, and there are plans for new sites in Saudi Arabia, Egypt, Kuwait, the Philippines, Vietnam and in nearly 200 other sites worldwide. The attraction of these shops includes the availability of matchday programmes before or just after matches and the "Theatre of Dreams" atmosphere which transports fans to pitchside at Old Trafford. Some of the larger stores will also have their own Red Cafés.

For the beginning of the 2000/2001 season, Manchester United's new Vodafone kit design was unveiled. You can order yours through the Megastore and online at **WWW.MANUTD.COM** – now you can look just like your favourite United stars, like Yorkey and Giggsy above!

On the NET!

If you have access to the internet, one of the must-see sites for all Manchester United fans is the club's official website – WWW.MANUTD.COM – Add it to your favourites!

With supporters all over the world, Manchester United has found a fantastic way to keep everyone, no matter where they are, up to date with all the latest news at Old Trafford. At WWW.MANUTD.COM you read match reports, buy official club merchandise, enter special competitions, have fun with MU Youth and a whole lot more, including:

- ALL THE LATEST NEWS
- MATCH PREVIEWS AND REVIEWS
- PLAYER PROFILES
- MANCHESTER UNITED MEGASTORE
- MU YOUTH (Featuring Fred the Red!)
- CONFERENCE AND CATERING FACILITIES
- VIRTUAL REALITY TOUR OF OLD TRAFFORD
- ALL THE RESULTS
- TICKET INFORMATION
- MUTV
- PLAYER POLLS

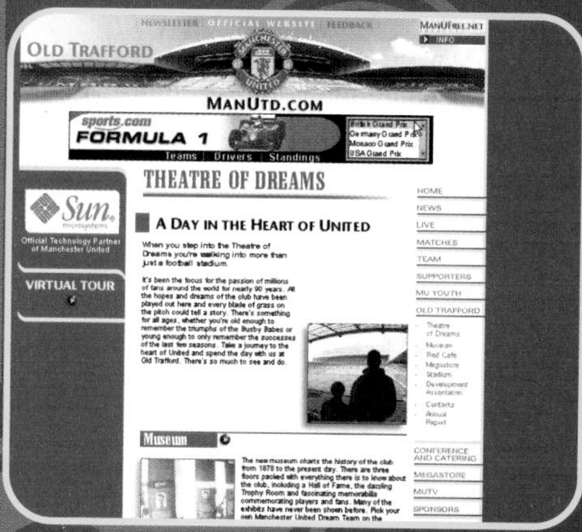

And of course, you can contact the club via e-mail and ask any questions you'd like to ask. You can also be added to the Manchester United e-mail list and be sent daily updates of what's going on at your club direct to your PC!

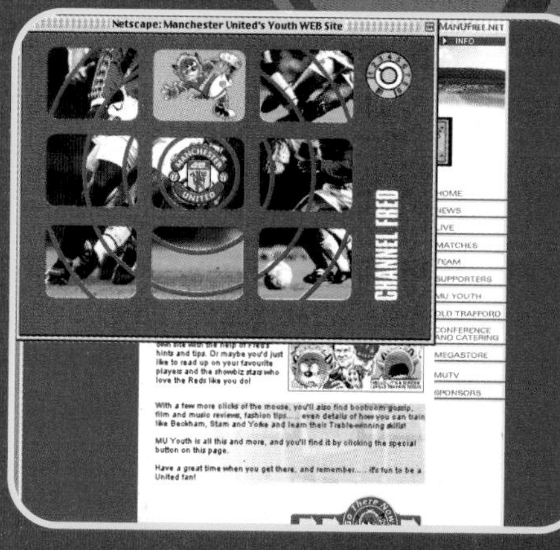

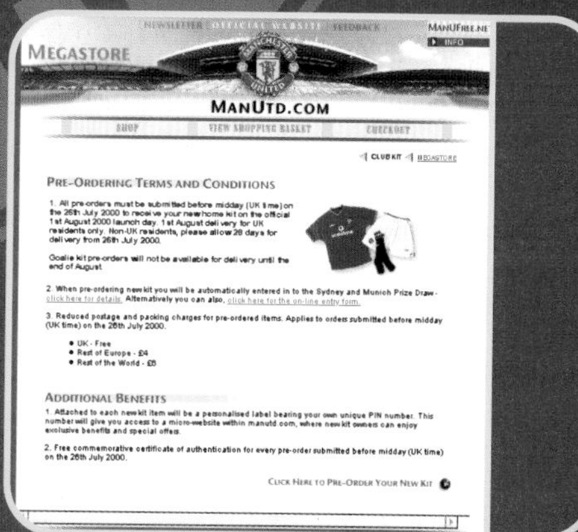

WWW.MANUTD.COM

– IT'S THE BEST WAY TO GO SURFING IN MANCHESTER!

SPOTTING THE STARS

One of the most satisfying things about United's success in recent years has been the important part played by the squad's youngsters. David Beckham, Paul Scholes, Ryan Giggs, Phil Neville, Nicky Butt and Gary Neville have all come through United's ranks - from schoolboys to the Youth Teams, onto the Reserves and then into the First Team itself. One of the greatest aspects of Sir Alex Ferguson's reign is that while he has spent large sums of money on bringing the cream of world footballing talent to the club, he has also successfully integrated the young stars and the established players into a world-beating team. With such great players being produced in the Youth Squads, the focus on training young players must continue!

The search for the "stars of the future" begins with children as young as nine, who receive at least 3 hours of intensive football coaching at United's impressive new Premier League Football Academy in Carrington. Competitive matches are organised between the United Academy and those from other Premier League clubs in many different age groups: Under-9s, Under-11s, Under-12s, Under-13s, Under-14s, Under-15s and Under-16s! Between 16 and 19 years of age, a player can receive a scholarship from the club as a trainee professional. At this stage, a player could represent United's famous and very successful Youth Team. Hopefully the player will then progress into the Reserve Team

HOW DO YOU GET SPOTTED?

The bottom line is: if you are good enough you will get spotted. Manchester United's scouts are all very experienced in judging a player's potential. They regularly watch selected games and players and there are plans to hold trials in the future. The best thing for a young player to do to get noticed, is to play for a top quality youth side or the local county side – these teams are the ones which are watched more often.

THE FA PREMIER LEAGUE ACADEMIES

In 1998, a new era of youth training was born. England's Centre of Footballing Excellence at Lilleshall was closed down and in its place, the Football Association (FA) required all Premier League Clubs to open their own Football Academies. Most of the bigger clubs already ran Centres of Excellence for their youth players but this new system was far bigger and better.

The Academy system was based on programmes that had been successfully running for years on the continent, especially in countries like Holland, and in South America. Nearly all Premier League Clubs now have prestigious new facilities for their Academies, as do some of the larger Nationwide League Clubs. Each club has its own system of selecting players for their Academies, but most use extensive scouting networks (Manchester United's is regarded as one of the very best) and open trials. Once a player has been spotted, he undergoes a 4-week selection process, at the end of which a decision is made as to whether he will continue at the Academy.

There are certain restrictions on how much time a youngster can spend travelling from home to the Academy. Children under 12 must live within one hour's driving time from the Centre, while those between 12 and 16 can live 1/2 hour further away.

OF THE FUTURE...

United's Reserve team celebrate winning the Manchester Senior Cup

United's Under-17 team in action against Crewe Alexandra

and a few continue into the First Team. Most of the current crop of home-grown United stars began their careers in this way.

Although it is obviously very exciting for any young lad to be involved in the Manchester United Academy, only a small percentage of these boys will go on to become professional footballers; and an even smaller proportion will get to play for United. However, if a young player is lucky enough to gain a place at the Manchester United Academy, he enjoys a number of benefits. There is a balanced education programme that helps the youngsters keep up with their school work and under the leadership of its Director, Les Kershaw, the Academy aims to provide:

- High Quality Coaching
- A Pleasant Working Environment
- A Comprehensive Welfare Service
- Medical and Physiotherapy Expertise
- A Close Working Relationship with Parents and Schools

Liverpool's Under-19s meet United's Under-19s

...THE HUNT GOES ON!

FRED THE RED

MANCHESTER UNITED'S YOUNGEST STAR PLAYER!

For all young Manchester United fans, Fred the Red is the fun side of Old Trafford. While the players and staff ensure Manchester United remain at the top of the world footballing table, Fred the Red and his friend Ro Rouge help keep United top of the fun charts too. Fred enjoys nothing better than getting out and about, meeting all his young fans. He signs autographs, laughs and jokes with celebrities and provides pre-match entertainment at Old Trafford, capering around the edge of the pitch, dancing to the music and generally enjoying himself before each match.

On match days, he has another important job to do – Fred is in charge of looking after the young mascots who accompany the teams onto the pitch and one of their best souvenirs of the day is their photograph with Fred. At half time, Fred once again entertains the crowd inside Old Trafford, but he has to be quick because before too long, the players will be out for the second half and he doesn't want to get into trouble with the referee!

Even on non-match days Fred is a very busy devil, a red one of course! As the official Manchester United mascot he is constantly in demand, visiting United stores all over the world for special events and personal appearances. For example, just before the United team flew to Brazil for the first ever FIFA World Club Championship, Fred joined Father Christmas at the Old Trafford Megastore to announce the winners of the competition which gave 20 fans the once-in-a-lifetime chance to go to Brazil to cheer on the lads. He was in great form and with Wes Brown also popping in, the event was a real treat for all those that were there – well done Fred! Keep a look out in official United publications and check out the club's website for details of when and where Fred the Red will make a personal appearance.

If you can't wait to see Fred the Red in person, take a look at our own special Fred the Red cartoon on Pages 24 and 25. Fred also finds time for a page in Glory Glory, United's official poster magazine, and in every United match programme there are Fred the Red competitions and a selection from Fred's massive postbag.

Of course, one of Fred's most important and most enjoyable jobs is answering all the fan mail he receives from young United fans from across the world. Have a look at the opposite page for some of the letters that have been sent to Fred at Old Trafford and if you've got something you want to send, go ahead! Fred's postman won't mind ... honest ... his bad back is getting much better!

If you have access to the internet you can visit Fred right now on the Official United website [see Page 58] at **WWW.MANUTD.COM/MUYOUTH** where you can find great puzzles, features, interviews, competitions and a whole lot more ... so go ahead and have some on-line fun with Fred the Red!

In off the Post!

Sir Alex Ferguson is great

I would like to congratulate Sir Alex Ferguson for the mighty works he has done as Manchester United Manager. Mr Ferguson is a great Manager whom I think is hard to replace. Look at the treble triumph, the Toyota Cup in Japan and the Championsup. In addition to this his players are regulars to their countries like David Beckham, Paul Scholes and Ryan Giggs and many more. Finally because I want to learn a lot from Manchester United I am looking for a pen-pal of both sex who scan keep me in touch with my favourite club

SIMBARASHE CHIKANYA
HOUSE NO 668
CHIKANGWE TOWNSHIP
KAROI
ZIMBABWE
AFRICA

This picture of David Beckham was sent in by Jack Watson (age 7)

Justine Roe
104 Gilman Street
Hanley.
Stoke-on-Trent
ST1 3PN

6/7/00

Dear pHill
Just being reading my issue of glory, glory, Man United and was really pleased to see the interview and poster of your new goalie. Fabien barthez. the poster is on my wall as I write this letter. I was wondering is there any chance I could get my hand's on a signed picture of the brilliant new goalie to add to my collection? I hope you can help. See all you red's soon.

Justine

Trymore Ben
House No. 401
Chanetsa cresent
Karoi
Zimbabwe
Africa

Dear Editor

My name is Trymore Ben,
I am a boy aged 16 and
I'm a Manchester United fan who keen in love with Manchester United Football Club since 1995. But because I live so far away from England / Old Trafford I did not get much news about Manchester United.
So if it is possible I would like any United pen-pals to write me back using this address above.

And my favourite players are David Beckham, Ryan Giggs, Dwight Yorke, Roy Keane, Andrew Cole, Gary Neville and Paul Scholes etc. etc. etc.
I wish you a good lucky to write me back.

Yours faithfully.

Trymore Ben

Fred the Red is always delighted to receive pictures, poems, stories, jokes - in fact everything and anything fun from young Manchester United fans all over the world. Here are some of the wonderful letters that have been sent to Fred recently. Please send your pictures, poems and jokes to Fred at the following address:

Fred the Red, Manchester United Football Club, Old Trafford, Manchester M16 0RA

Answers

Page 5 – SPOT the BALL

ANSWER: THE BALL HAS BEEN REMOVED FROM SQUARE F1

Page 13 – UNITED WORD GRID

ANSWER: THE PHRASE REVEALED IS "UNITED ARE THE CHAMPIONS"

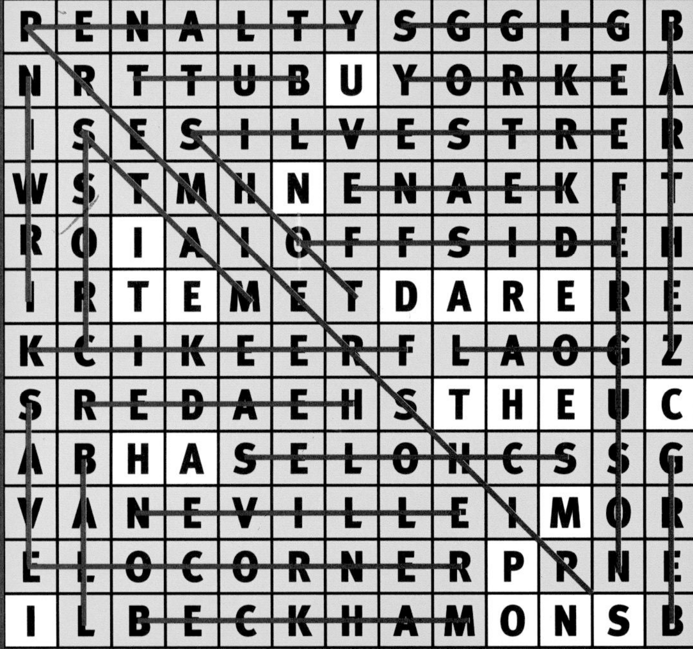

Page 17 – WHO ARE YA?

ANSWERS:

1. HENNING BERG
2. OLE GUNNAR SOLSKJAER
3. DWIGHT YORKE
4. ROY KEANE
5. TEDDY SHERINGHAM
6. RYAN GIGGS

Page 30/31 – UNITED CROSSWORD

ANSWER: UNITED WERE PREVIOUSLY KNOWN AS NEWTON HEATH

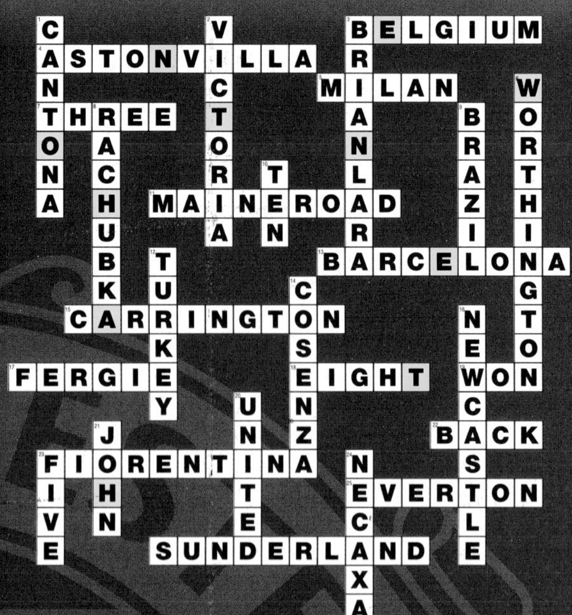

Page 40/41 – SO, YOU THINK YOU KNOW UNITED?

PART ONE: NICE AND EASY!

1. BROOKLYN
2. PHIL NEVILLE
3. BAYERN MUNICH
4. NOTTINGHAM
5. ABERDEEN
6. THE RED DEVILS
7. RYAN GIGGS AGAINST ARSENAL
8. MARK BOSNICH
9. SCORPIO
10. TUNISIA

PART TWO: CHALLENGING STUFF!

1. BOBBY CHARLTON
2. NEIL SULLIVAN
3. STADE DE FRANCE, PARIS
4. DAVID BECKHAM AGAINST NECAXA
5. ARSENAL – 2-1 IN THE CHARITY SHIELD AT WEMBLEY, 1/8/1999
6. JAAP STAM
7. SHE IS VICTORIA ADAMS, 'POSH SPICE' FROM THE WORLD FAMOUS POP GROUP THE SPICE GIRLS
8. 45 GOALS
9. BRYLCREEM
10. SOUTH AFRICAN

PART THREE: THE REAL TEST

1. NOTTINGHAM FOREST
2. SIR MATT BUSBY
3. ARROWS
4. ANDREI KANCHELSKIS
5. NETBALL
6. ERIC CANTONA
7. ALAN SHEARER, IAN WRIGHT, LES FERDINAND, ROBBIE FOWLER AND MATT LE TISSIER
8. 13th POSITION IN 1990
9. ANDY COLE, ROY KEANE AND DWIGHT YORKE. GABRIEL BATISTUTA SCORED FOR FIORENTINA
10. UNITED HAVE ONLY HAD SEVEN (7) MANAGERS SINCE 1945: SIR MATT BUSBY (1945-69; 1971-72), WILF MCGUINNESS (1969-70), FRANK O'FARRELL (1971-72), TOMMY DOCHERTY (1972-77), DAVE SEXTON (1977-81), RON ATKINSON (1981-86), SIR ALEX FERGUSON (1986-)

PLAYING AWAY!

ARSENAL – HIGHBURY
ASTON VILLA – VILLA PARK
BRADFORD CITY – VALLEY PARADE
CHARLTON ATHLETIC – THE VALLEY
CHELSEA – STAMFORD BRIDGE
COVENTRY CITY – HIGHFIELD ROAD
DERBY COUNTY – PRIDE PARK
EVERTON – GOODISON PARK
IPSWICH TOWN – PORTMAN ROAD
LEEDS UNITED – ELLAND ROAD
LEICESTER CITY – FILBERT STREET
LIVERPOOL – ANFIELD
MANCHESTER CITY – MAINE ROAD
MIDDLESBROUGH – RIVERSIDE STADIUM
NEWCASTLE UNITED – ST JAMES' PARK
SOUTHAMPTON – THE DELL
SUNDERLAND – STADIUM OF LIGHT
TOTTENHAM HOTSPUR – WHITE HART LANE
WEST HAM UNITED – THE BOLEYN GROUND

Page 45 – SHAPE UP

1. RYAN GIGGS
2. JAAP STAM
3. ROY KEANE
4. ANDY COLE